First World War
and Army of Occupation
War Diary
France, Belgium and Germany

20 DIVISION
59 Infantry Brigade,
Brigade Machine Gun Company
23 February 1916 - 27 February 1918

WO95/2117/3

The Naval & Military Press Ltd
www.nmarchive.com
Published in association with The National Archives

Published by

The Naval & Military Press Ltd

Unit 10 Ridgewood Industrial Park,

Uckfield, East Sussex,

TN22 5QE England

Tel: +44 (0) 1825 749494

www.naval-military-press.com

www.nmarchive.com

This diary has been reprinted in facsimile from the original. Any imperfections are inevitably reproduced and the quality may fall short of modern type and cartographic standards.

© Crown Copyright
Images reproduced by permission of The National Archives, London, England, 2015.

Contents

Document type	Place/Title	Date From	Date To
Heading	WO95/2117 20 Division 59 Infantry Brigade (3) Brigade Machine Gun Company Feb 1916-Feb 1918		
Heading	20th Division 59th Infy Bde 59th Machine Gun Coy. Feb 1916-Feb 1918 (Diary For December 1916 Missing)		
Heading	59th Brigade 20th Division. Disembarked Havre 25.2.16 59th Machine Gun Company 23.2.16 To 2.3.16 Feb 18		
War Diary	Grantham	23/02/1916	23/02/1916
War Diary	Southampton	24/02/1916	24/02/1916
War Diary	Le Havre	25/02/1916	01/03/1916
War Diary	Brandhoek	02/03/1916	02/03/1916
Heading	59th Brigade. 20th Division. 59th Machine Gun Company March 1916		
War Diary	Brandhoek	03/03/1916	05/03/1916
War Diary	Yser Canal Bank	06/03/1916	07/03/1916
War Diary	Canal Bank	08/03/1916	30/03/1916
War Diary	Billets	31/03/1916	31/03/1916
Heading	59th Brigade. 20th Division. 59th Machine Gun Company April 1916		
War Diary	Billets	03/04/1916	03/04/1916
War Diary	Canal Bank	08/04/1916	13/04/1916
War Diary	Billets	15/04/1916	16/04/1916
War Diary	Houdtkerque	17/04/1916	17/04/1916
War Diary	Wormhoudt	18/04/1916	25/04/1916
War Diary	Houdtkerque	26/04/1916	26/04/1916
Heading	59th Brigade. 20th Division. 59th Machine Gun Company May 1916		
Miscellaneous	From O.C. 59 Machine Gun Company	04/06/1916	04/06/1916
War Diary	Calais	07/05/1916	07/05/1916
War Diary	Zoodkirke	14/05/1916	14/05/1916
War Diary	Bollezeele	15/05/1916	15/05/1916
War Diary	Winnezeele	16/05/1916	16/05/1916
War Diary	Houdkerque	20/05/1916	20/05/1916
War Diary	Brandthoek	22/05/1916	22/05/1916
War Diary	Canal Bank	27/05/1916	29/05/1916
Heading	59th Brigade. 20th Division. 59th Machine Gun Company June 1916		
War Diary	Canal Bank	01/06/1916	02/06/1916
War Diary	Ypres	03/06/1916	08/06/1916
War Diary	St Jean	16/06/1916	26/06/1916
Heading	59th Inf. Bde. 20th Div. War Diary 59th Machine Gun Company July 1916		
War Diary	Brandhoek	01/07/1916	01/07/1916
War Diary	St Jean	05/07/1916	10/07/1916
War Diary	Wormhout	16/07/1916	16/07/1916
War Diary	Petit Pont	19/07/1916	19/07/1916
War Diary	Locre	24/07/1916	24/07/1916
War Diary	Brevillers	25/07/1916	25/07/1916
War Diary	Brandhoek	01/07/1916	01/07/1916

War Diary	St Jean	05/07/1916	10/07/1916
War Diary	Wormhout	16/07/1916	16/07/1916
War Diary	Petit Pont	19/07/1916	19/07/1916
War Diary	Locre	24/07/1916	24/07/1916
War Diary	Brevillers	25/07/1916	25/07/1916
War Diary	Brandhoek	01/07/1916	01/07/1916
War Diary	St. Jean	05/07/1916	10/07/1916
War Diary	Wormhout	16/07/1916	16/07/1916
War Diary	Petit Pont	19/07/1916	19/07/1916
War Diary	Locre	24/07/1916	24/07/1916
War Diary	Brevillers	25/07/1916	25/07/1916
War Diary	Authie	27/07/1916	27/07/1916
War Diary	Hebouterne	28/07/1916	30/07/1916
War Diary	Authie	27/07/1916	27/07/1916
War Diary	Hebouterne	28/07/1916	30/07/1916
Heading	59th Brigade. 20th Division. 59th Brigade Machine Gun Company August 1916		
War Diary	Hebuterne	01/08/1916	14/08/1916
War Diary	Authie	18/08/1916	18/08/1916
War Diary	Beauval	19/08/1916	19/08/1916
War Diary	Happy Valley	20/09/1916	20/09/1916
War Diary	Briqueterie	21/09/1916	25/09/1916
War Diary	Briqueterie	26/08/1916	30/08/1916
Heading	59th Brigade. 20th Division. 59th Machine Gun Company September 1916		
War Diary	Craters (Nr Carnoy)	01/09/1916	01/09/1916
War Diary	Briqueterie	02/09/1916	03/09/1916
War Diary	Guillemont	04/09/1916	04/09/1916
War Diary	Happy Valley	05/09/1916	05/09/1916
War Diary	Carnoy Bois Des Tailles	06/09/1916	06/09/1916
War Diary	Corbie	08/09/1916	08/09/1916
War Diary	Bois Des Tailles	11/09/1916	11/09/1916
War Diary	Bromfay Fm.	14/09/1916	14/09/1916
War Diary	Ginchy	15/09/1916	17/09/1916
War Diary	Meaulte	20/09/1916	20/09/1916
War Diary	Morlancourt	21/09/1916	23/09/1916
War Diary	Happy Valley	25/09/1916	25/09/1916
War Diary	Guillemont	26/09/1916	26/09/1916
War Diary	Happy Valley	27/09/1916	28/09/1916
Heading	59th Brigade. 20th Division. 59th Machine Gun Company October 1916		
War Diary	Carnoy	01/10/1916	01/10/1916
War Diary	Guedecourt	04/10/1916	06/10/1916
War Diary	Trones Wood	07/10/1916	07/10/1916
War Diary	Meaulte	09/10/1916	09/10/1916
War Diary	Treux	10/10/1916	14/10/1916
War Diary	Franvillers	19/10/1916	19/10/1916
War Diary	Cardonette	20/10/1916	20/10/1916
War Diary	Yzeux	21/10/1916	31/10/1916
Heading	59th Brigade. 20th Division. 59th Machine Gun Company November 1916		
War Diary	Yzeux	01/11/1916	01/11/1916
War Diary	Ailly-Sur-Somme	02/11/1916	02/11/1916
War Diary	Saissemont.	03/11/1916	14/11/1916
War Diary	Ailly-Sur-Somme	15/11/1916	15/11/1916
War Diary	Ville-Sur-Ancre	16/11/1916	29/11/1916

Heading	War Diary of The 59th Machine Gun Company January 1917 Vol XI		
War Diary	Maltzhorn Valley	31/12/1916	31/12/1916
War Diary	Coy Hdqrs Haie Wood Near Combles	01/01/1917	01/01/1917
War Diary	Haie Wood	02/01/1917	12/01/1917
War Diary	Bronfay Farm	13/01/1917	20/01/1917
War Diary	Haie Wood	21/01/1917	25/01/1917
War Diary	Bronfay Farm	26/01/1917	26/01/1917
War Diary	Franvillers	27/01/1917	30/01/1917
Heading	War Diary 59th M.G. Company February 1917 Vol 12		
War Diary	Franvillers	31/01/1917	04/02/1917
War Diary	La Houssoye	05/02/1917	06/02/1917
War Diary	Mansel Camp	07/02/1917	07/02/1917
War Diary	Guillemont	08/02/1917	28/02/1917
Heading	War Diary of 59th Bde. Machine Gun Company For March 1917		
War Diary	Briquetterie Near Montauban	01/03/1917	01/03/1917
War Diary	Briquetterie	02/03/1917	05/03/1917
War Diary	Guillemont	06/03/1917	18/03/1917
War Diary	Briquetterie Near Montauban	19/03/1917	19/03/1917
War Diary	Briqueterie	20/03/1917	25/03/1917
War Diary	Saille-Saillisel	26/03/1917	28/03/1917
War Diary	Mesnil-En-Arrouaise.	29/03/1917	30/03/1917
Heading	War Diary 59th Machine Gun Company April 1917 Vol 14		
War Diary	Canal Station P.32.b.1.8. Map 57c S.E.	31/03/1917	05/04/1917
War Diary	Rocquiney	06/04/1917	13/04/1917
War Diary	Ytres	14/04/1917	14/04/1917
War Diary	Ruyaulcourt	15/04/1917	25/04/1917
War Diary	Bertincourt	26/04/1917	27/04/1917
War Diary	Ytres	29/04/1917	29/04/1917
Heading	59 M G Coy War Diary May 1916 59th M.G. Company Vol 15		
War Diary	Ytres	30/04/1917	03/05/1917
War Diary	P.29.a.3.7	04/05/1917	07/05/1917
War Diary	P.29.a.3.7. Map. 57c N E	08/05/1917	09/05/1917
War Diary	P.29.a.3.7.	10/05/1917	10/05/1917
War Diary	P.29.a.3.7. Map. 57c N.E.	10/05/1917	10/05/1917
War Diary	Havrincourt Wood	11/05/1917	15/05/1917
War Diary	Avramcourt Wood	16/05/1917	20/05/1917
War Diary	Nauville Bonseuruval	21/05/1917	21/05/1917
War Diary	Le Transloy	22/05/1917	22/05/1917
War Diary	Favreuil	23/05/1917	23/05/1917
War Diary	C.22.d.6.4.	24/05/1917	27/05/1917
War Diary	Beugnatre	28/05/1917	30/05/1917
Heading	War Diary of 59th Coy. M.G.C. June 1917 Vol 16		
War Diary	Beugnatre	31/05/1917	06/06/1917
War Diary	Noreuil	07/06/1917	21/06/1917
War Diary	Beugnatre	22/06/1917	23/06/1917
War Diary	Gomiecourt	24/06/1917	26/06/1917
War Diary	Gomiecourt	27/06/1917	28/06/1917
War Diary	St Leger-Les-Domart	29/06/1917	29/06/1917
Heading	War Diary 59th Machine Gun Coy. July 1917 Vol 17		
War Diary	St Leger-Les-Domart	29/06/1917	29/06/1917
War Diary	St Leger	30/06/1917	20/07/1917
War Diary	Canada	21/07/1917	23/07/1917

War Diary	Dragon Camp	24/07/1917	15/08/1917
War Diary	Malakoff Farm	15/08/1917	18/08/1917
War Diary	Proven	19/08/1917	30/08/1917
War Diary	Pilch Camp	31/08/1917	08/09/1917
War Diary	Elverdinghe	09/09/1917	18/09/1917
War Diary	Malakoff Farm	19/09/1917	29/09/1917
War Diary	Proven Area	30/09/1917	30/09/1917
War Diary	Pilch Camp	01/10/1917	01/10/1917
War Diary	Beaulencourt	02/10/1917	06/10/1917
War Diary	Heudicourt	07/10/1917	07/10/1917
War Diary	In The Field Nr Gouzeaucourt	08/10/1917	08/10/1917
War Diary	Gouzeaucourt	09/10/1917	30/10/1917
Heading	War Diary 59th Machine Gun Coy. November 1917 Vol 21		
War Diary	Gouzeaucourt	31/10/1917	05/11/1917
War Diary	Heudicourt	06/11/1917	12/11/1917
War Diary	Gouzeaucourt	13/11/1917	21/11/1917
War Diary	In The Field	22/11/1917	24/11/1917
War Diary	Gouzeaucourt	25/11/1917	29/11/1917
War Diary	Near Lateau Wood	30/11/1917	30/11/1917
War Diary	Heudicourt	04/12/1917	04/12/1917
Operation(al) Order(s)	59 M.G. Coy. O.O. No. 4	18/11/1919	18/11/1919
War Diary	Campagne	12/12/1917	07/01/1918
War Diary	La Clyte	08/01/1918	11/01/1918
War Diary	In The Line Menin Rd Sector	12/01/1918	17/01/1918
War Diary	La Clytte Camp	18/01/1918	24/01/1918
War Diary	Line	29/01/1918	29/01/1918
War Diary	La Clytte Camp	30/01/1918	01/02/1918
War Diary	In The Line Menin Road Sector	04/02/1918	12/02/1918
War Diary	La Clytte	13/02/1918	20/02/1918
War Diary	Avricourt	27/02/1918	27/02/1918
Miscellaneous	H.Q. 20th Division	06/04/1918	06/04/1918

WO 95/2117

20 Division
59 Infantry Brigade
Brigade Machine Gun Company

(3)

Feb 1916 – Feb 1917

20TH DIVISION
59TH INFY BDE

59TH MACHINE GUN COY.

FEB 1916- FEB 1918.

(DIARY FOR DECEMBER 1916 MISSING)

59th Brigade.
20th Division.

Disembarked Havre 25.2.16.

59th MACHINE GUN COMPANY

23.2.16 to 2.3.16.

Feb '18

(Dec '16 Missing)

Army Form C. 2118.

WAR DIARY
or
INTELLIGENCE SUMMARY.
(Erase heading not required.)

59 M.G. Coy.

Instructions regarding War Diaries and Intelligence Summaries are contained in F. S. Regs., Part II. and the Staff Manual respectively. Title pages will be prepared in manuscript.

Place	Date	Hour	Summary of Events and Information	Remarks and references to Appendices
GRANTHAM	23.2.16		Marched off from BELTON PARK about 10 pm, & entrained at the MILITARY SIDING. Left about 11.35 pm	
SOUTHAMPTON	24.2.16		Arrived SOUTHAMPTON about 10 am, & detrained at POINT 23. Capt BIRCH & 2nd Lts AITKEN, STURSBERG, HOWARD & MACGILLIVRAY embarked on SS MARGUERITE at QUAY No 50 with Nos 1,2 & 4 Sections. Lts EARLE & 2nd Lt HAMMERTON, BUSCKE & MOGG embarked on SS ARCHIMEDES with No 3 Section & transport. SS MARGUERITE sailed about 9.0 pm, but SS ARCHIMEDES was held back thro' submarines in the ENGLISH CHANNEL.	
LE HAVRE	25.2.16		Arrived LE HAVRE at about 6.0 am. Disembarked at 8.0 am. Proceeded to REST CAMP No 5.	
LE HAVRE	26.2.16		At 9.0 am Coy proceeded thro' LE HAVRE to REST CAMP No 2.	
LE HAVRE	27.2.16 28.2.16		Awaited arrival of remainder of Coy in SS ARCHIMEDES	
LE HAVRE	1.3.16		SS ARCHIMEDES arrived about 4.0 am. Coy marched to the QUAY & entrained at GARE MARITIME. Left about 8.0 pm	
BRAND HOEK	2.3.16		Arrived POPERINGHE about 6.0 pm. Proceeded by the YPRES ROAD to BRANDHOEK, where the Coy was billeted in huts	

59th Brigade.
20th Division.

59th MACHINE GUN COMPANY

MARCH 1916

WAR DIARY — INTELLIGENCE SUMMARY

59 M.G. Coy.

Army Form C. 2118.

Place	Date	Hour	Summary of Events and Information	Remarks and references to Appendices
BRANDHOEK SIDG	3/6.3.16		Prepared for proceeding to trenches	
CANAL BANK	6.3.16 / 7.3.16		Proceeded via VLAMERTINGHE to dug-outs in YPSER CANAL BANK by LEICESTER BRIDGE	
CANAL BANK	8.3.16		Took over emplacements at THE WILLOWS, LONG WILLOW, FOCH FARM, WILSON'S FARM, IRISH FARM (X10), X9, MACGREGOR'S POST & TOWER POST. Nos 3 & 4 relieved by No 1 Sec, & remainder by No 2.	
CANAL BANK	9.3.16 / 30.3.16		Relief takes place every 4 days. After second relief guns & gun teams in X9 removed to emplacement at CROSS ROADS FARM in front line trenches. Every evening 4/8 guns (generally 6) were used for indirect fire on enemy's support trenches, trolley crossings and other points of strategic importance. About 85,000 rds used. Pte AITKEN went sick 22.3.16 & left by ambulance 4 am 23.3.16 followed by 6 M.G. Coy. & proceeded to BILLETS and exception of 2 gun teams under Pt TURNBERG, which proceeded to L2 Defences.	
BILLETS	31.3.16			

A.J.

59th Brigade.
20th Division.

59th MACHINE GUN COMPANY

APRIL 1916

59 M.G. Coy.

Army Form C. 2118.

WAR DIARY
INTELLIGENCE SUMMARY
(Erase heading not required.)

Instructions regarding War Diaries and Intelligence Summaries are contained in F.S. Regs., Part II. and the Staff Manual respectively. Title pages will be prepared in manuscript.

Vol 2

Place	Date	Hour	Summary of Events and Information	Remarks and references to Appendices
BILLETS	3.4.16		2 gun teams in LA DÉTENTES relieved by M.M.G.C.	
CANAL BANK	8.4.16		100 men from 60 M.G. Coy new employment in CONEY STREET to which the teams for THE WILLOWS was transferred. Relieved the other 2 employments.	
CANAL BANK	13.4.16		2/Lt BARLOW (60 WILTS REGT) arrived	
BILLETS	15.4.16		Relieved by No 16 M.G. Coy, proceeding to billets between 10.0pm & 2.30am.	
BILLETS	16.4.16		8 men arrived as reinforcements from Grantham.	
HOUDKERQUE	17.4.16		Proceeded from billets through POPERINGHE to HOUDKERQUE, the Coy being billeted in farms (officers) + farmhouses.	
WORMHOUDT	18.4.16		Marched ahead of 59 BDE to billets between WORMHOUDT & CASSEL, arriving about 4.30pm.	
WORMHOUDT	20.4.16		32 men arrived for instruction from the BDE (8 from each Bn.)	
WORMHOUDT	21.4.16		Instructional class commenced under Mr. TURSBERG	
WORMHOUDT	25.4.16		Inspection by G.O.C. 59th Bde.	
HOUDTKERQUE	21.4.16		Moved back to HOUDTKERQUE, occupying the same billets as on 17.4.16	C.O.J.

59th Brigade.
20th Division.

59th MACHINE GUN COMPANY

M A Y   1 9 1 6

To The D.A.G.
   3rd Eschelon
      Rouen.

From O.C. 59 Machine Gun Company.

4-6-16

    Herewith, original War Diary of above Company for May 1916.

In Field,
4-6-16.

                       J.C.A. Birch. Major
                       COMDG. No. 59. M.G. COY.
                       MACHINE GUN CORPS.

Army Form C. 2118.

WAR DIARY
or
~~INTELLIGENCE SUMMARY.~~
(Erase heading not required.)

Instructions regarding War Diaries and Intelligence Summaries are contained in F.S. Regs., Part II. and the Staff Manual respectively. Title pages will be prepared in manuscript.

Place	Date	Hour	Summary of Events and Information	Remarks and references to Appendices
CALAIS	7.5.16		Left HOUTKERQUE about 5.0am proceeded to POPERINGHE, there entraining for CALAIS. Arrived about 7.30pm. Retained & proceeded to LARGE REST CAMP by BELGIAN AVIATION GROUND.	
ZOODKIRKE	13.5.16		Left CALAIS late afternoon 13.5.16 & proceeded to ZOODKIRKE, occupying hutten at LAFONTAIRE. 14.5.16	
BOLLEZEELE	15.5.16		Left ZOODKIRKE about 10 am & proceeded to BOLLEZEELE. Arrived about 4pm & went into billets. 15.5.16	
WINNEZEELE	16.5.16		Left BOLLEZEELE about 11.0 am & proceeded to WINNEZEELE Arrived about 5.30pm & went into billets.	
HOUDKERQUE	19.5.16		Left WINNEZEELE 19.5.16 & proceeded to Old billets at HOUDKERQUE	
BRANDHOEK	22.5.16		Left HOUDKERQUE 21.5.16 at 5.30am & proceeded to rest & hut up BRANDHOEK, arriving there about 10.15 am.	
CANAL BANK	27.5.16		Took over from 61 M.G.Coy. on night of 26/27.5.16. who had previously relieved G.Guards M.G.Coy.	
"	28.5.16		Pte R.HEMMINGS (No5123) wounded in left side on 27.5.16.	
"	29.5.16		2357 Pte I.F. BRETT killed on night of 28.5.16.	

59th Brigade.
20th Division.

59th MACHINE GUN COMPANY

JUNE 1916

59 M.G. Coy.
59/MGC 28
Army Form C. 2118.
JUNE
Vol 4

WAR DIARY

INTELLIGENCE SUMMARY

(Erase heading not required.)

Place	Date	Hour	Summary of Events and Information	Remarks and references to Appendices
CANAL BANK	1.6.16	—	Coy in the line with Hqrs in CANAL BANK/ Run ybs from DEAD END/ 1st Coy.	
"	2.6.16	—	Wounded 3949 Pte J. HUTCHINSON, 5256 A. POWELL, 559 J. DOUGHERTY & 5252 J. BAILY while unloading limbers at DEAD END/	
YPRES	3.6.16	—	Moved to billets in YPRES/	
"	6.6.16	—	Wounded 5212G. ALBUTT & 5287 E.A. SPINNER three bursting of 77 outside Belgian Sector Arm POTIJZE WOOD/	
"	8.6.16	—	Killed Pte ALLEN & BLATCH wounded Sgt SPINKS, L/Cpl RIDGEWAY, Pte WILLOUGHBY & recd. Thro' bombardment of M.G. Emplacements in ST JEAN	
ST JEAN	16.6.16	—	Coy HQ moved to ST JEAN.	
"	17.6.16	—	Killed Sgt COCHRANE, Wounded Cpl EDWARDS, Pte TYLER thro' bombardment of own trenches & adjoining houses (see map ref. for 8.6.16)	
"	29.6.11	—	Wounded Pte HETHERUM L. MAY.	
"	1.6.16	—	During bombardment of ST JEAN L/Cpl "B" in evening 8 Pte WELLINGTON & MEGARRTY & L GRAHAM wounded & 1 BATTALION wounded on WELLINGTON ROAD/	

Kinsley ...
59 M.G.C.

59th Inf.Bde.
20th Div.

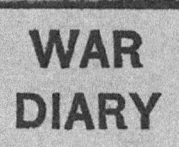

59th MACHINE GUN COMPANY.

J U L Y

1 9 1 6

59 M.G. Coy.
20 59 M.G. Coy
Army Form C/2118.
Vol 5

To: H.Q. XX Division

Herewith War Diary for month of July of 59th M.G. Co.

Allyunly/lr
O.C. 59 M.G.Co.
1/8/16

HEAD QUARTERS, 20th DIVISION.
Date 1.8.16

Place	Date	Hour	Summary	Remarks and references to Appendices
BRANDHOEK	1.7.16	—	Coy in rest billets	
ST JEAN	5.7.16	—	Coy relieved 61st Coy being in trenches in … sector, … wounded	
ST JEAN	10.7.16	—	… at POTIJZE in (HAYMARKET) Com & BARNWICK … particularly newly trench behind … BKY & WELLINGTON	
WORMHOUT	16.7.16	—	Relieved by M.G. by tram & … to WORMHOUT	…ceeded from YPRES … thence by train
PETIT PONT	19.7.16	—	Left WORMHOUT, … over from 72 M.G.C.	to NEUVE EGLISE, taking … day
LOCRE	24.7.16	—	Relieved by 118 M.G.Coy on night 23/24 & Coy kept at PETIT PONT then marched to LOCRE being billeted in huts. The Coy was turned out by 5th BORDER REGT & went to billets at ECOLE DE LA SAINTE FAMILLE	
BRÉMETZ	25.7.16	—	Marched from LOCRE to POPERINGHE & entrained there. Arrived at FREVENT	

59 M G Coy
20 59 M G Coy
Army Form C/2118.
VOL 5

Instructions regarding War Diaries and Intelligence Summaries are contained in F. S. Regs., Part II. and the Staff Manual respectively. Title pages will be prepared in manuscript.

(Erase heading not required.)

Place	Date	Hour	Summary of Events and Information	Remarks and references to Appendices
BRANDHOEK	1.7.16	—	Coy in rest billets at BRANDHOEK (Coy transport lines)	
ST JEAN	5.7.16	—	Coy relieved 61 MG Coy on night of 5/6 July, distributions as before. Sector same being in ST JEAN + POTIZJE. Dvr BEBBINGTON wounded	
ST JEAN	10.7.16	—	Trench raid on night of 10/11 July. Very severe retaliation, particularly at POTIZJE No 2 Gun (a gun in an occupied assembly trench behind HAYMARKET) Casualties. Pte PALMER killed, Cpls QUAY + WELLING wounded. Sgt BARNICK wounded, Pte BAIRD shell shock	
WORMHOUT	18/7/16	—	Relieved by MG Coy (6th Division) on night of 7/15/16 July. Proceeded from YPRES by train + slept in camp near proceeded from thence by train to WORMHOUT, occupying German billets	
PETIT PONT	19.7.16	—	Left WORMHOUT, marched to HERZEELE + proceeded by bus to NEUVE EGLISE, taking over from 72 MG Coy (Coy HQ PETIT PONT). Dr Killanny died	
LOCRE	24.7.16	—	Relieved by 118 MG Coy on night of 23/24 July. Left at PETIT PONT the personnel to LOCRE, being billeted in huts. The Coy was turned out by 5th BORDER REGT + went to billets at ECOLE DE LA SAINTE FAMILLE	
PROVEN(?)	25.7.16	—	Marched from LOCRE to POPERINGHE + entrained there. Arrived at PROVEN	

Army Form C. 2118.

59 M.G. Coy. Certified true copy
Chundley M.

WAR DIARY
or
INTELLIGENCE SUMMARY.
(Erase heading not required.)

Instructions regarding War Diaries and Intelligence Summaries are contained in F.S. Regs., Part II. and the Staff Manual respectively. Title pages will be prepared in manuscript.

Place	Date	Hour	Summary of Events and Information	Remarks and references to Appendices
BRANDHOEK	1.7.16	—	Coy in rest billets at BRANDHOEK (Coy transport Hoo.)	
ST JEAN	5.7.16	—	Coy relieved 61 M.G.Coy on night of 5/6 July, dispositions as before, Hoo. Hrs hqrs in ST JEAN POTIJZE. 2/Cpl BERRINGTON wounded.	
ST. JEAN	10.7.16	—	Trench raid on night of 10/11 July. Very severe retaliation, particularly on POTIJZE and NO LEE (4 guns in mocked up assembly trench behind HAYMARKET) Casualties: Pte PALMER killed, Cpl QUAY & WELLING, Pte BARWICK wounded, Pte BIRD shell shock.	
WORMHOUT	16.7.16	—	Relieved by M.G.Coy (6th Division) on night of 16/17.16 July. Proceeded from YPRES by horse & left in Coy transport lines. Proceeded from the train to WORMHOUT occupying previous billets.	
PETIT PONT	19.7.16	—	Left WORMHOUT, marched to HERZEELE & proceeded by train to NEUVE EGLISE, taking over from 72 M.G.Coy (Coy Hqrs. PETIT PONT). [illegible] following day.	
LOCRE	24.7.16	—	Relieved by 118 M.G.Coy on night of 23/24 July. Left for PONT PONT. Then marched to LOCRE, being billeted in huts. The Coy was mounted by 5th BORDER REGT & went to billets at ECOLE DE LA SAINTE FAMILLE.	
BRANVILLERS	25.7.16	—	Marched from LOCRE to PAPERINGHE, entrained there. Arrived at PREVENT	

Army Form C. 2118.

WAR DIARY
INTELLIGENCE SUMMARY.
(Erase heading not required.)

59 M.G.Coy.

Place	Date	Hour	Summary of Events and Information	Remarks and references to Appendices
Contd			about 9.0 p.m. marched to MILLENCOURT. Coy billeted in CHATEAU	
AUTHIE	27.7.16		Marched to AUTHIE. Coy billeted close to D.A.C. Transport Lines.	
HEBOUTERNE	28.7.16		Coy marched to HEBOUTERNE. Coy H.Qrs at SAILLY-AUX-BOIS. Took over from 114 M.G.Coy.	
HEBOUTERNE	30.7.16		Coy H.Qrs moved from SAILLY-AUX-BOIS to No.3 Puller, HEBOUTERNE.	

O Strudergam.

59 MG Coy

Copy

Army Form C. 2118.

WAR DIARY
or
INTELLIGENCE SUMMARY.
(Erase heading not required.)

Instructions regarding War Diaries and Intelligence Summaries are contained in F. S. Regs., Part II. and the Staff Manual respectively. Title pages will be prepared in manuscript.

Place	Date	Hour	Summary of Events and Information	Remarks and references to Appendices
Curlu			About 9.0 p.m. marched to billets at BREVILLERS. Coy billeted in Chateau.	
AUTHIE	27.7.16	—	Marched to AUTHIE. Coy billeted close to D.A.C. Transport lines.	
HEBUTERNE	28.7.16	—	Coy marched to HEBUTERNE. Coy H.Qrs at SAILLY-AUX-BOIS. Took over from 114 M.G.Coy.	
HEBUTERNE	30.7.16	—	Coy Hqrs moved from SAILLY-AUX-BOIS to No 3 Billet, HEBUTERNE.	

O Churchley 2/Lt

59th Brigade.
20th Division.

59th BRIGADE MACHINE GUN COMPANY

AUGUST 1916.

59 M.G. Coy Aug 1916. Vol 6 20/

WAR DIARY or **INTELLIGENCE SUMMARY**
Army Form C. 2118.

Place	Date	Hour	Summary of Events and Information	Remarks and references to Appendices
HÉBUTERNE	1.8.16		In the line on HÉBUTERNE, with 10 guns in line & 6 in reserve	
"	4.8.16		MAJOR J.C.A BIRCH returned to England after handing Coy over to LT J.Y SCOTT	
			10 R.B. Coy then made emplacements & dugouts consolidated front	
			line in preparation for attack until 18.8.16	
AUTHIE	18.8.16		Coy left HÉBUTERNE spent night in billets near AUTHIE	
BEAUVAL	19.8.16		Coy moved to billets in BEAUVAL	
			CAPT. H. MASON, WARWICKSHIRE REGT attd M.G.C.	
HAPPY VALLEY	20.9.16		Coy moved by rail from CANDAS to MÉRICOURT going into bivouacs in "HAPPY VALLEY"	
BRAQUETERIE	21.9.16		Coy went into the line in front of GUILLEMONT. Coy HQrs BRAQUETERIE	
"	23.9.16		Wounded: A/Cpl JONES, Pte HUDSON. Sgt QUESNÉ held up infantry	
			which had retired from front line owing to enemy attack returned	
			them to their Coy Commander. Recommended & awarded for A.C.M.	
"	24.9.16		Killed: Pte MATTHEWS, Pte HOGARTH GEORGE, Wounded: A/Cpl COPE, Pte HALEY PATERSON	Signed J.Y Scott
"	26.9.16		Killed in BIVOUACS, Wounded: Pte LLOYD (5788), BROWNETT, JAMES. Wounded	
			subsequently died of wounds: Cpl QUAY	

59 M.G.Coy. Aug 1916.

WAR DIARY
or
INTELLIGENCE SUMMARY.
(Erase heading not required.)

Army Form C. 2118.

Place	Date	Hour	Summary of Events and Information	Remarks and references to Appendices
BRAQUETERIE	26.8.16		Killed Mc Pherson	
"	27.8.16		Wounded Ptes Owings, Butterfield, Drake, Johnson	
"	28.8.16		Wounded Col Reid, Ptes Westfall, Allain, Hope	
"	29.8.16		Wounded Sgt Isles, Ptes Turner, Gatehen, Wyse, Davidson, Ptes Ingland + Statham Sgt Welling	
"	30.8.16		Coy relieved by 61 M.G.Coy. went to dugouts on the Citadel.	

59th Brigade.
20th Division.

59th MACHINE GUN COMPANY

SEPTEMBER 1 9 1 6

59 M.G.Coy ①

Army Form C. 2118.

50th Machine Gun Company Vol 7

WAR DIARY
or
INTELLIGENCE SUMMARY
(Erase heading not required.)

Place	Date	Hour	Summary of Events and Information	Remarks and references to Appendices
CRATERS (nr CARNOY) BAZIQUETERIE	1.9.16	—	Coy at THE CRATERS	
	2.9.16	—	Went into line at own dpt in front of GUILLEMONT, orders received for capture of GUILLEMONT next day	
"	3.9.16	—	ZERO 12.0 midday. 4 Secs on right (Mr HOWARD + Mr EVANS) + 3 Sec on left (Mr HAMMERTON + 2Lr CORNISH) in front line. 1 Sec (Mr FP MACGILLIVRAY + Mr BUSCH) in support + 2 Secs (Lt STURBERG) in reserve. About 11.30 a.m. Mr CORNISH had a miraculous bad accident (but killed 1 wounded, Mr CORMITZ orderly buried but unwounded). All No 9 Sec remaining half of No 3 went over with 4th wave of infantry. Mr EVANS wounded in head soon after. Report received that 1st objective had been taken + No 1 Sec was moved up to see Coy H.Q. (ARROWHEAD LANE — so far behind English front line). Near CEMETERY, GUILLEMONT, 4 HAMMERTON killed by shell. Remainder of advanced support gave advanced with infantry. Arrived in final objective (500 yds E of GUILLEMONT). No Sec engaged knocked out an enemy M.G. detachment on opposite side of valley. Reserve guns (No 2 Sec) arrived in new ground fire about M.i.i hour after arrival of infantry + dug in at once. NOT. The night was spent with disturbance.	Sturberghi

Army Form C. 2118.

WAR DIARY
or
INTELLIGENCE SUMMARY.
(Erase heading not required.)

157 M.G.Coy

Instructions regarding War Diaries and Intelligence Summaries are contained in F.S. Regs., Part II. and the Staff Manual respectively. Title pages will be prepared in manuscript.

Place	Date	Hour	Summary of Events and Information	Remarks and references to Appendices
GUILLEMONT	4.9.16	/	(4 M.G.Coy) Lt McCLEARTY & Mr HARVEY, in each with 4 guns, sent up by GOC 59 Bde to reinforce. Mr HARVEY sent to shell-hole near CEMETERY, & Lt McCLEARTY relieved Lt TURNER in front line, who took up defensive line behind to the East of GUILLEMONT, where A/M Coy Hqrs had been dug. Lt EARLE (Shell-shock) & Mr BUSCAS (dysentery) sent back, Lt STURSBERG took over acting 2nd i/c of Coy. Positions held all day under heavy shelling, 3 machine-guns lost and Sgt CASSIDY (i/c remaining half of No 3. Sec.)	
HAPPY VALLEY	5.9.16	/	Relieved at early dawn by 48 M.G.Coy (2nd army) back to HAPPY VALLEY.	
BRAY ON BOIS DES TAILLES	6.9.16	/	Moved to BOIS DES TAILLES (between BRAY & CORBIE). Mr HOWARD recommended for M.C. & Sgt QUEENS for D.C.M. Roll call showed	Offrs Other Ranks KILLED 1 12 WOUNDED 3 42 SHELL SHOCK 2 4
CORBIE	8.9.16	/	Proceeded to CORBIE, went into billets. Mr DAVENHILL rejoined Coy on 10.9.16. Sgt CASSIDY also back, wind up now.	
BOIS DES TAILLES	11.9.16	/	Returned to tents & huts in BOIS DES TAILLES. Mr TILLEY & Lt DRAPER joined Coy.	
BRUMPAY FM.	14.9.16	/	Marched to HAPPY VALLEY, repair nights near BRUMPAY FARM.	
GINCHY	15.9.16 17.9.16	/	Moved into line arriving about dawn am 16th. Mr ABRAHAMS joined Coy.	3rd Gds Bde.
MEAULTE	20.9.16	-	Relieved by 3rd Gds Bde M.G.G, & proceeded by G.S. wagons to SANDPITS, MÉAULTE.	
MORLANCOURT	21.9.16	-	Moved to huts, MORLANCOURT.	
	22.9.16	-	Lt CRAWSHAW joined Coy as 2nd i/c.	O. F. Morgan

Army Form C. 2118.

WAR DIARY
or
INTELLIGENCE SUMMARY.
(Erase heading not required.)

Instructions regarding War Diaries and Intelligence Summaries are contained in F. S. Regs., Part II. and the Staff Manual respectively. Title pages will be prepared in manuscript.

Place	Date	Hour	Summary of Events and Information	Remarks and references to Appendices
MORLANCOURT	23.9.16	—	Capt Masury proceeded to ENGLAND on 8 days special leave.	
HAPPY VALLEY	25.9.16	—	Moved to HAPPY VALLEY.	
GUILLEMONT	26.9.16	—	Moved into trenches 1 August near ARROW HEAD COPSE, GUILLEMONT in reserve.	
HAPPY VALLEY	27.9.16	—	Relieved by French & went back to HAPPY VALLEY.	
"	28.9.16	—	M.C. D.C.M. for Mr HOWARD & Sgt QUESNEL respectively.	

59th Brigade.
20th Division.

59th MACHINE GUN COMPANY

OCTOBER 1 9 1 6

59 M.G.C. October 1916

WAR DIARY
INTELLIGENCE SUMMARY
(Erase heading not required.)

Army Form C. 2118.

Place	Date	Hour	Summary of Events and Information	Remarks and references to Appendices
CARNOY	1.10.16	—	Coy in tents in Divisional Reserve in CARNOY VALLEY	
GUEUDECOURT	4.10.16	—	Relieved 61 M.G. Coy night 4/5th in sight of GUEUDECOURT. 4 guns in line, but subsequently 4 reserve sent up. 9.9 into support line. Casualties: Wounded: Pte KNIGHTS	
	5.10.16	—	NORMAL.	
GUEUDECOURT	6.10.16	—	Wounded Dr HALL (subsequently died of wounds CQJ)	
TRONES WOOD	7.10.16	—	Coy relieved by 14 M.G. Coy proceeded to bivouacs at TRONES WOOD. Casualties: Wounded at CplMORDEN	
MEAULTE	9.10.16	—	Proceeded to MEAULTE having handed over to 1st DIVISION. Coy in same billets as before.	
TRÉUX	10.10.16	—	Proceeded to billets in TRÉUX by 29th Division H.Q.	
TRÉUX	18.10.16	—	Lt CRANSTOWN proceeded on leave to U.K.	
FRANVILLERS	19.10.16	—	2Lt J.L. HOWARD proceeded on leave to U.K. Coy moved to billets at FRANVILLERS PRAM.	
CARDONETTE	20.10.16	—	Lt Col MOGG killed at CARDONETTE. Coy moved into billets at CARDONETTE. Commanded by ??	
YZEUX	23.10.16	—	Coy moved into billets at YZEUX being billeted with 59 S.M.B. at the Chateau.	
	31.10.16	—	Coy is still in billets at YZEUX.	

Allrowoofed
Capt ?????
of ??????

59th Brigade.
20th Division.

59th MACHINE GUN COMPANY

NOVEMBER 1916

WAR DIARY
or
INTELLIGENCE SUMMARY.
(Erase heading not required.)

Army Form C. 2118.

59 M G Coy
Vol 9

Place	Date	Hour	Summary of Events and Information	Remarks and references to Appendices
YZEUX.	1-11-16		Left YZEUX 9-0 A.M. Coy arrived AILLY-SUR-SOMME 12-30 P.M. when it billeted for the night. Divisional General inspected Coy on line of march. Roads in good condition. WEATHER:— FINE.	WD for 59 M G Coy later by
AILLY-SUR-SOMME	2-11-16		Coy left AILLY-SUR-SOMME at 10.0 A.M. for SAISSEMONT arriving about 11:30 A.M. Put accommodation. WEATHER:— WET.	
SAISSEMONT.	3-11-16 TO 12-11-16		This period was spent by the Coy in Autumn Training which included training of recruits, tactical exercises, G.H.Q. O.B. 181. dated 13-10-16 stating that 8 O.R. from Battalions in the Brigade were to be transferred to M.G. Coys to make a higher establishment of 174 O.R.s Transports were also increased by one limber G.S. and two G.D. horses. WEATHER:— INDIFFERENT	WD for
SAISSEMONT.	13-11-16		Inspection by 4th ARMY COMMANDER GENERAL RAWLINSON. Coy complimented on general smartness. WEATHER:— FINE.	WD for
SAISSEMONT	14-11-16		Received orders from Bde Hdqrs 12-0 noon to proceed to AILLY-SUR-SOMME immediately. Arrived 3-4-5 P.M. Received O.O. to proceed to the Somme. WEATHER:— FINE.	WD for

Army Form C. 2118.

WAR DIARY
or
INTELLIGENCE SUMMARY.
(Erase heading not required.)

Instructions regarding War Diaries and Intelligence Summaries are contained in F. S. Regs., Part II. and the Staff Manual respectively. Title pages will be prepared in manuscript.

Place	Date	Hour	Summary of Events and Information	Remarks and references to Appendices
AILLY-SUR-SOMME	15-11-16		Coy left AILLY-SUR-SOMME at 10:0 AM on motor lorries (FRENCH) for VILLE -SUR-ANCRE. Arrived 12-15 P.M. WEATHER:- COLD & FINE.	
VILLE ANNY-S.R-ANCRE	16-11-16		Coy training in the morning. Half holiday in the afternoon. WEATHER:- COLD & FINE.	
VILLE ANNY-SUR-ANCRE	17-11-16		Coy firing on range. Bathing in the afternoon. WEATHER:- COLD & FINE.	
VILLE-SUR-ANCRE	18-11-16		Coy training. WEATHER: WET.	
VILLE-SUR-ANCRE	14-11-16		Coy training. Range practice. I.A. McLaren.	
	22-11-16		WEATHER. WET.	
VILLE-S-ANCRE	23-11-16		Coy manœuvres with Tactical exercises. Roads in a very bad state. Motor lorries etc prevented from passing certain places owing to bad roads.	
	29-11-16		WEATHER:- "INDIFFERENT"	

War Diary Vol XI
of the
5th Machine Gun Company
January 1917

WAR DIARY
or
INTELLIGENCE SUMMARY
(Erase heading not required.)

Army Form C. 2118.

Place	Date	Hour	Summary of Events and Information	Remarks and references to Appendices
MALTZHORN VALLEY	31st Dec/16		Coy left CORBIE for MALTZHORN VALLEY CAMP at 9.0 AM by motor-bus. Bell Major 59th Bay/Bee informed 2nd in command just before leaving CORBIE that the 'front' had been changed. Coy arrived at MALTZHORN VALLEY about 1-30 PM. 2nd in Comd then proceeded up the line to make all new arrangements. Camp was in a very bad condition; men & officers suffers considerably and no tent boards. WEATHER DULL	What's 59 M.G.Y
Coy Hdgrs HAIE WOOD NEAR COMBLES	1st Jan. 1917		Coy left MALTZHORN CAMP at 1-30 PM arriving at new Hdgrs about 3-10 PM and proceeded to relieve 2nd & 3rd Guards Bde M.G. Coys. Guards had a guide for each gun team. men had tea before proceeding further. all snipping and belt boxes taken over. 13 guns employed and two for emergency fire, at night Relief completed about 3-35 PM. Left Group Bell Hdgrs at BOIS DORES. WEATHER DULL	
HAIE WOOD	2nd Jan./17		Coy in the line. a great deal of work required to be done to make the men comfortable. Men in "line" for 6 days and then went for emergency 2 days, section at refuge improved. One section in reserve at Coy Hdgrs who relieves the enemy other night in a cycle. No casualties. WEATHER DULL	

Army Form C. 2118.

WAR DIARY
or
INTELLIGENCE SUMMARY
(Erase heading not required.)

Instructions regarding War Diaries and Intelligence Summaries are contained in F.S. Regs., Part II. and the Staff Manual respectively. Title Pages will be prepared in manuscript.

Place	Date	Hour	Summary of Events and Information	Remarks and references to Appendices
HAIE WOOD	3rd Jan/17		2/Lt. DAVENHILL admitted to hospital. R.E.'s working at emplacements and dug-outs. WEATHER. WET.	
HAIE WOOD	4th Jan/17		Twenty men reinforcements arrived from base. One man killed. WEATHER FINE.	Nom. Rolls 69 M.G.Coy
HAIE WOOD	5th Jan/17		Enemy aircraft active all day. Two of Coy's machine guns fired at them. 3. O.R. admitted to hospital sick. WEATHER FINE	
HAIE WOOD	6th Jan/17		9 nominal firing was used with 2 guns 3000 rounds fired. Target — German trench. Results unknown. German machine guns on a enemys very active. No casualties. WEATHER. DULL	
HAIE WOOD	7th Jan/17		Maj. or MASON, M.C. commanding 59 M.G.Coy. ordered to report to School of Instruction CAMIERS. 2 non Coms assumed temporary command of Coy from post completed in B.R.O. Left Base group sick - shipped to the night for 300 ↑. WEATHER. DULL	
HAIE WOOD	8th Jan/17		R.E.'s building emplacements and dug outs in support line. Our artillery bombing enemy front lines for	

2449 Wt. W14957/M90 750,000 1/16 J.B.C. & A. Forms/C.2118/12.

WAR DIARY
or
INTELLIGENCE SUMMARY

Army Form C. 2118.

Place	Date	Hour	Summary of Events and Information	Remarks and references to Appendices
HAIE WOOD	8th Jan/17	3/4 an hour	Enemy artillery quiet. WEATHER. WET.	M.C. for 59 M.G. Cny
HAIE WOOD	9th Jan/17		Machine gun with two guns on suspected enemy Hqrs at COON COPSE range 3000. Result unknown. 2. O.R. admitted to hospital sick. Enemy artillery quiet.	
HAIE WOOD	10th Jan/17		Bde notified as that 60th M.G. Coy would relieve us in the line on the night of 11/12. The adjutant to S. WEATHER. SNOW. Again assumed command of the Coy. WEATHER. COLD. Relief postponed until night 12/13. Enemy artillery normal. No casualties. 1 officer reinforcement arrived. WEATHER. WET.	
HAIE WOOD	11th Jan/17			
HAIE WOOD	12th Jan/17		Ordered to leave all No1's "limbs" with unit minus of the 13th. 60 Coy arrived about 3.30 P.M. The quick firing gun detailed. All tripods & belt boxes taken away by them. 7 hay. Leaving the same number of each at BRONFAY FARM CAMP. 108. Relief complete at about 8.15 P.M. with its exception of No1's left behind. Coy proceeded by Section to March	

WAR DIARY
or
INTELLIGENCE SUMMARY

(Erase heading not required.)

Army Form C. 2118.

Instructions regarding War Diaries and Intelligence Summaries are contained in F. S. Regs., Part II. and the Staff Manual respectively. Title Pages will be prepared in manuscript.

Place	Date	Hour	Summary of Events and Information	Remarks and references to Appendices
HAIE WOOD	12th Jan/17	9am	to BRONFAY FARM CAMP 108. No casualties. Enemy artillery quiet. WEATHER. WET	Wwtr 59M.G.Cy
HAIE WOOD to BRONFAY FARM	13th Jan/17	9am	Coy resting and cleaning equipment etc. WEATHER. DULL.	
BRONFAY FARM.	14th Jan/17	9am	Half the Coy on fatigues at Railhead. It is extremely difficult to obtain differences on L get guns etc in good order. Remainder of Coy cleaning up. WEATHER. DULL.	
BRONFAY FARM	15th Jan/17	9am	Forty six men on fatigues. Remainder improving camp. WEATHER. DULL	
BRONFAY FARM.	16th Jan/17	9am	Coy training. WEATHER. DULL	
BRONFAY FARM.	17th Jan/17	9am	Coy training. Kit inspection & deficiencies taken. WEATHER. SNOW.	

Army Form C. 2118.

WAR DIARY
or
INTELLIGENCE SUMMARY
(Erase heading not required.)

Instructions regarding War Diaries and Intelligence Summaries are contained in F. S. Regs., Part II and the Staff Manual respectively. Title Pages will be prepared in manuscript.

Place	Date	Hour	Summary of Events and Information	Remarks and references to Appendices
BRONFAY FARM.	18th Jan/17		C.O. inspects the tin hats to be taken over. Lectures on bombing by Bell. Working in tailors. Coy on fatigue in the morning.	WWI.Sh. 59MGCoy
BRONFAY FARM.	19th Jan/17		O.O. received to relieve 61 M.G. Coy on the night 20th/21st. The whole Coy on fatigue all day.	WEATHER. SNOW.
BRONFAY FARM.	20th Jan/17		Coy preparing for the "hive" in the morning. Coy moved off at 12·30 P.M. for HAIE WOOD arriving there about 3·30 P.M. Route taken was through MARICOURT. HARDECOURT J. MAUREPAS. Coy relieved 61 M.G. Coy by 11·30 P.M. 13 guns in the line, with stores at Coy H.dqrs. and HAIE WOOD. One of them being used stone for A.A. work. No casualties. Enemy artillery very quiet. All supplies and half-hours taken over. Arrival. Roads in a very good condition. Snow lay on the ground much heavy front at night. Coy in the night group and WEATHER. SNOW.	
HAIE WOOD	21st Jan/17		Coy in the line. Two hostile aeroplanes were engaged at different times during the day by our A.A. G.G.s.	

Army Form C. 2118.

WAR DIARY
or
INTELLIGENCE SUMMARY
(Erase heading not required.)

Instructions regarding War Diaries and Intelligence Summaries are contained in F. S. Regs., Part II. and the Staff Manual respectively. Title Pages will be prepared in manuscript.

Place	Date	Hour	Summary of Events and Information	Remarks and references to Appendices
HAIE WOOD	21/1/17	CONT'D	They were seen to turn. Enemy M.G. was firing along the main PERONNE – BAPAUME road at about 9-30 P.M. using "indirect fire." One of our M.G's fired about 3500 rounds on tracks ENE about GOVERNMENT FARM, and on tracks N of ST. PIERRE VAAST WOOD from about midnight to 4-0 A.M. in the hope of catching enemy relief. Result unknown. Firing to the frosty nature of the weather, men are not using "gun boots though." WEATHER:– FROST.	War W/- 59 M.G. Coy
HAIE WOOD	22-1-17		Enemy artillery firing rather heavily, fired on and about the CHATEAU in SAILLY-SAILLISEL between 5-0 to 5-30 P.M. no damage. Our artillery bombarded the front line system of enemy trenches opposite our sub-sector about 2-0 P.M. to 3 P.M. with good effect. No casualties either on the 21 or 22 Jan. or to-day. WEATHER:– FROST.	

WAR DIARY
INTELLIGENCE SUMMARY
(Erase heading not required.)

Army Form C. 2118.

Place	Date	Hour	Summary of Events and Information	Remarks and references to Appendices
HAIE WOOD	23-1-17		Enemy artillery fairly quiet. Two machine guns were in evidence, method firing at intervals during the night on enemy tracks. No casualties in the Coy. WEATHER FROST.	MG by 59 M.G. Coy
HAIE WOOD	24-1-17		Two enemy aeroplanes brought down by A.A. gun during the morning. Enemy artillery shelled HAIE WOOD road near the Cemetery & COMBLES, inflicting a few casualties on men and animals. Enemy also shelled the vicinity of RE dump at HAIE WOOD, a few casualties. Enemy shelled off & into yards during the night. Received O.O.[?] relief in the night 25/26" Jan. 79.17. No casualties in the Coy. WEATHER FROST.	
HAIE WOOD	25-1-17		Coy relieved, with no casualties. [?] and half hour taken over an usual. On relief Coy proceeded to Camp 108 at BRONFAY FARM. Enemy artillery fairly active. During this tour in the trenches it has extremely difficult to keep the guns in condition as enemy threw the guns broke up. Glycerine received was used	

2449 Wt. W14957/M90 750,000 1/16 J.B.C. & A. Forms/C.2118/12

Army Form C. 2118.

WAR DIARY
or
INTELLIGENCE SUMMARY
(Erase heading not required.)

Instructions regarding War Diaries and Intelligence Summaries are contained in F. S. Regs., Part II. and the Staff Manual respectively. Title Pages will be prepared in manuscript.

Place	Date	Hour	Summary of Events and Information	Remarks and references to Appendices
HAIE WOOD	25-1-17		hut was found to be of very little use. It practically collapsed by the Coy on to fire single shot every few minutes and a wasp's nest coming in somewhere. WEATHER FROST.	H.Q. 4/59 M.G.Coy
BRINFAY FARM	26-1-17		Coy entrained at 12·0 NOON. for FRANVILLERS arriving at about 2 P.M. Billets were shot away 9·00. WEATHER FROST.	
FRANVILLERS	27-1-17		Coy cleaning up equipment etc. and repacking limbers. No.1 SECTION. proceeded under 2/Lt DRAPER to FLESSELLES for A.A. work.	WEATHER FROST.
FRANVILLERS	28-1-17		Owing to bad accommodation here Coy were ordered to proceed to HEILLY. This was cancelled just before Coy moved. Men of the Coy fitted out with new clothing.	WEATHER FROST
FRANVILLERS	29-1-17		Coy training.	WEATHER FROST
FRANVILLERS	30-1-17		Coy training.	WEATHER FROST

Vol 12

War Diary
59th M.G. Company
February 1917

Army Form C. 2118.

WAR DIARY
or
INTELLIGENCE SUMMARY

(Erase heading not required.)

Instructions regarding War Diaries and Intelligence Summaries are contained in F. S. Regs., Part II. and the Staff Manual respectively. Title Pages will be prepared in manuscript.

Place	Date	Hour	Summary of Events and Information	Remarks and references to Appendices
FRANVILLERS	31st Jan: 17		Coy training. No casualties in hospitals etc. WEATHER: FROST.	AHQ. 1r 59 M.G.Coy
FRANVILLERS	1st Feb:1917		Coy training. One man evacuated to C.C.C.S sick. One man shot himself through the foot whilst cleaning his rifle. WEATHER FROST.	
FRANVILLERS	2nd Feb:17		Coy training. One Cpl & Seven O.R's evacuated to C.C.S Sick. WEATHER: FROST	
FRANVILLERS	3rd Feb:17		Coy inspected by O.C. 20th Div. WEATHER. FROST.	
FRANVILLERS	4th Feb:17		Coy moved to LA HOUSSOYE camp about 11-45 A.m. Got a field for the men. The following morning received during the morning: A high wind began rain. At 5.30 p.m. yesterday (3rd) enemy shewed heavy bombardment on front part of high ground south east of RANCOURT and followed it up with an infantry attack on and	

WAR DIARY
INTELLIGENCE SUMMARY

Army Form C. 2118.

Place	Date	Hour	Summary of Events and Information	Remarks and references to Appendices
FRANVILLERS	4th Feb. 1917	Con'd	Enemy were driven off by our rifle + artillery fire aaa. All now quiet aaa. Our lines intact aaa Raid seems to have been made on left Divn. of Corps on our right, report no attack both places on its front aaa ends. At 11 P.M. 3rd we attacked 2 (two) lines of German trenches mmmm River Ancre N.W. of Grandcourt from R.8.6.8.4 to R.26.0.6. aaa. All objectives attained gained aaa Casualties slight aaa Prisoners 1 officer 200 O.R. 3 Machine Guns. WEATHER. STUFFROST.	1st C.Rt.L.I 59N.9.C9
LA HOUSSOYE	5th Feb. 1917		Coy preparing for the "Line". Guns were inspected up to stores + old kettles owing to scarcity of match. WEATHER. FROST.	
LA HOUSSOYE	6th Feb. 1917		Coy left billets 9-a.m. in busses for Mansel Camp. arriving about 12-45 P.M. Men in tents. WEATHER FROST.	

WAR DIARY
or
INTELLIGENCE SUMMARY

(Erase heading not required.)

Army Form C. 2118.

Place	Date	Hour	Summary of Events and Information	Remarks and references to Appendices
MANSEL CAMP	7th Feb 1917		CONTD Coy left MANSEL CAMP 11:45 AM and proceeded to GUILLEMONT where 88th M.G. Coy moving 4 PM relief completed casualties nil.	7pm 2nd 17 M.G.Coy
GUILLEMONT	8th Feb 1917		LT. CRANSHAW had 6/14 DRAPER left for M.G. School CAMIERS. WEATHER - FROST Front was quiet, no casualties	
GUILLEMONT	9th Feb 1917		WEATHER - FROST One (1) Man wounded in face M.G. fire. Two (2) O.R. sick to hospital WEATHER - FROST	
GUILLEMONT	10th Feb 1917		LT. MACGILLIVRAY returned from course at M.G. school CAMIERS. 2 offrs & 15 OR arrived from the base WEATHER - FROST	
GUILLEMONT	11th Feb 1917		2nd Bn relief took place. no casualties. WEATHER - FROST	
GUILLEMONT	12th Feb 1917		62372 Pte Bargo EH evacuated for F.G.C.M. No casualties in trenches WEATHER - FROST	
GUILLEMONT	13th Feb 1917		No casualties. 2/Lt. N. CORNISH sick to hospital. WEATHER - FROST	
GUILLEMONT	14th Feb 1917		Sector heavily shelled during the early part of the night. A large carrying party from the coy were caught, and two (2) OR severely wounded, and two (2) slightly wounded by shrapnel WEATHER - FROST	

Army Form C. 2118.

WAR DIARY
or
INTELLIGENCE SUMMARY
(Erase heading not required.)

Instructions regarding War Diaries and Intelligence Summaries are contained in F. S. Regs., Part II. and the Staff Manual respectively. Title Pages will be prepared in manuscript.

Place	Date	Hour	Summary of Events and Information	Remarks and references to Appendices
GUILLEMONT	15th Feb 1917	CONT'D	No Casualties. Two (2) OR sick to hospital. WEATHER - FROST	Appx 4. 59 MGC
GUILLEMONT	16th Feb 1917		Inter Section relief took place, no casualties. Two (2) OR sick to hospital. WEATHER - FROST	
GUILLEMONT	17th Feb 1917		No casualties. Two (2) OR returned from hospital. WEATHER - THAW & RAIN	
GUILLEMONT	18th Feb 1917		One (1) OR to hospital. One (1) OR wounded by shrapnel. WEATHER - RAIN	
GUILLEMONT	19th Feb 1917		About 6 PM enemy advanced and captured the most advanced infantry post on the brigade front. Later action relief was in progress and all guns took up defensive positions about reserve and support lines but were not called upon. No casualties. 62372 Pte Banyo E.H. was tried by F.G.C.M. at GUILLEMONT. WEATHER - RAIN	
GUILLEMONT	20th Feb		No casualties. 1. OR sick to hospital. WEATHER - DULL	

Army Form C. 2118.

WAR DIARY
or
INTELLIGENCE SUMMARY
(Erase heading not required.)

Instructions regarding War Diaries and Intelligence Summaries are contained in F. S. Regs., Part II. and the Staff Manual respectively. Title Pages will be prepared in manuscript.

Place	Date	Hour	Summary of Events and Information	Remarks and references to Appendices
GUILLEMONT	21st Feb. 1917		One of the left forward gun positions received a direct hit with a 5.9 Trench Mortar, but no casualties in gun team. Two O.R. wounded by shrapnel and 1 O.R. sick to hospital. Trenches in a very bad state at present owing to WEATHER - DULL and RAIN.	S.M.G.(y)
GUILLEMONT	22nd Feb 1917		No casualties. Condition of trenches same. WEATHER - DULL	
GUILLEMONT	23rd Feb 1917		Inter section relief took place during night. Casualties nil. 1 O.R. sick to hospital. WEATHER - RAIN	
GUILLEMONT	24th Feb 1917		No Casualties WEATHER - DRY & DULL	
GUILLEMONT	25th Feb 1917		Lt. C.D. STURSBERG returned to duty next coy, on being relieved of duties as a/Town Major at FRANVILLERS. No Casualties. WEATHER - DULL	
GUILLEMONT	26th Feb 1917		Three (3) O.R. proceeded to Course at CAMIERS, 1 O.R. sick to Hospital. WEATHER - FAIR.	

Army Form C. 2118.

WAR DIARY
or
INTELLIGENCE SUMMARY
(Erase heading not required.)

Instructions regarding War Diaries and Intelligence Summaries are contained in F. S. Regs., Part II. and the Staff Manual respectively. Title Pages will be prepared in manuscript.

Place	Date	Hour	Summary of Events and Information	Remarks and references to Appendices
GUILLEMONT	27th Feb 1917		One (1) O.R. wounded by shrapnel. Two (2) O.R. sick to hospital. Lt. H.H. CRAWSHAW and 2/Lt T. DRAPER returned from course at CAMIERS. Reinforcement of three (3) O.R. arrived from base. WEATHER – FAIR.	From 31.MGCy
GUILLEMONT	28th Feb 1917	At 5.25 AM	the Bde. attempted a minor operation. Two platoons advanced but getting caught up in uncut wire, suffered heavy casualties and were compelled to return. This Coy. together with the guns of the 60th M.G. Coy. shook hot and climbed our guns at rock platoon during the night, put over a heavy M.G. barrage in rear trenches. Average expenditure of S.A.A. eleven (11) belts per gun. In the evening the guns of this Coy. were withdrawn and the Coy. returned to huts at BRIQUETERIE. Relief completed by 2.30 AM. Casualties Nil.	

SECRET.

WAR DIARY OF 59th Bde.
MACHINE GUN COMPANY
FOR
MARCH 1917.

Place	Date	Hour	Summary of Events and Information	Remarks and references to Appendices
BRIQUETERIE (Near Wariencourt)	1st April	Morning	Coy. returns in the morning. Cleaning equipment etc. in the afternoon. WEATHER DULL.	W.D. [?] 59 M.G.Coy
BRIQUETERIE	2nd April 1917		Coy. cleaning guns and equipment all day. WEATHER DULL.	
BRIQUETERIE	3rd April 1917		Coy. training. WEATHER FINE.	
BRIQUETERIE	4th April		Coy. training. WEATHER FINE with SNO[W]	
BRIQUETERIE	5th April		Coy. training. No 2 Section proceeded to the intermediate line and took up positions in V.12 V.5.Y.2. XIV Corps was composed of two Divisions only, 20th Div. & Guards Division. Owing to the repeated movement of the enemy on this Transloy front, "G" Group (3rd Div.) took Battles on their retirement from the Durcocq. O.O received to relieve 60 M.G.Coy in the line on this my [?] March. WEATHER FINE.	

Army Form C. 2118.

WAR DIARY
or
INTELLIGENCE SUMMARY
(Erase heading not required.)

Instructions regarding War Diaries and Intelligence Summaries are contained in F. S. Regs., Part II and the Staff Manual respectively. Title Pages will be prepared in manuscript.

Place	Date	Hour	Summary of Events and Information	Remarks and references to Appendices
GUILLEMONT	6th March 1917		Coy baths in the morning and the preparing for the two Coy had their first workup with gas mask. Perfect system with the hut at GUILLEMONT. 60 Coy was relieved by about 10.30 PM with no casualties. Twelve guns in at time the 58 Sea Section went line were relieved by 60 Coy in the night 28/1st March 1917. Casualties 1 OR (SICK) WEATHER FINE.	W.O. L. 59th Div.
GUILLEMONT	7th March		Coy in the line. Enemy artillery below normal. No casualties. WEATHER DULL.	
GUILLEMONT	8th March		No casualties. Enemy quiet. WEATHER DULL.	
GUILLEMONT	9th March		Incinerator fire was used on enemy trenches STUTTGART and MORTAR LANE. Results unknown owing to mist. 1500. B.4 gun moved up to No.3 position (Range wind). Enemy artillery below normal. No casualties. 2 OR reinforcements from BASE reported. WEATHER DULL.	

Army Form C. 2118.

WAR DIARY
or
INTELLIGENCE SUMMARY
(Erase heading not required.)

Instructions regarding War Diaries and Intelligence Summaries are contained in F. S. Regs., Part II. and the Staff Manual respectively. Title Pages will be prepared in manuscript.

Place	Date	Hour	Summary of Events and Information	Remarks and references to Appendices
GUILLEMONT	10th March 1917		Indirect-fire during the night upon MORTAR LANE. 1000 rounds fired. Results unknown. Inter station relief carried out on night 10/11th. No casualties. Enemy artillery normal. WEATHER FINE.	11 C.Cp 59 MGCy
GUILLEMONT	11th March		Indirect-fire on MORTAR LANE & junction of trenches N36 93 1000 rounds fired. FALL & BENNET trenches shelled between 10 AM & 11.30 AM. Enemy machine guns active on night - breakthroughs & vicinity of SUNKEN ROAD between 5.0 AM & 6.0 AM and 6.0 PM & 9.0 PM. Casualties 10.R. (Shrapnel). WEATHER FINE.	
GUILLEMONT	12th March		Indirect-fire on some Targets as last night. Rumours from c/1000. Enemy artillery active. Anti aircraft emp. bombardment built at OX. TRENCH. Casualties Major OR (SICK) 1 Officer reinforcement carried from Base. WEATHER DULL.	
GUILLEMONT	13th March		Intentional relief carried out. Indirect fire on MORTAR LANE and trenches in that area. 2000 rounds fired. Also 1000 rounds upon trenches and tracks NORTH of WURTEMBURG CONTd	

2449 Wt. W14957/M90 750,000 8/16 J.B.C. & A. Forms/C.2118/12.

WAR DIARY or INTELLIGENCE SUMMARY

Army Form C. 2118.

Place	Date	Hour	Summary of Events and Information	Remarks and references to Appendices
GUILLEMONT.	13th March 1917	Cont'd	Enemy artillery normal. Casualties: nil I.O.R. (SICK) WEATHER. DULL	MacL— 59 M.G. Coy
GUILLEMONT.	14th March		Indirect fire from FALL upon WURTEMBURG TRENCH. to backs to NORTH and upon MORTAR LANE and reversely 3000 rounds fired. One gun in ANTELOPE TRENCH fired until the mid-change. Gun in NO.3. position turned during enemy retaliation. Our bombardment. Then three since been recovered. Enemy sent up both flares bursting into two green lights which exploded into a significan artillery to open fire on the checkerboards. Casualties: nil I.O.R. (SICK). Enemy artillery normal. WEATHER. WET	
GUILLEMONT	15th March		Indirect fire upon MORTAR LANE. WURTEMBOURG & STUTTGART trenches, 200 rounds fired. Results unknown. Gun in MERCIER trench turned. Dug-out blown in on a gun turnel. Enemy artillery normal. Casualties I.O.R. (SICK) WEATHER. FINE	

WAR DIARY
or
INTELLIGENCE SUMMARY

Army Form C.2118.

Place	Date	Hour	Summary of Events and Information	Remarks and references to Appendices
GUILLEMONT	16th March 1917		Enemy trench active with M.G's rifle grenades and artillery all day & night. Casualties NIL. WEATHER FINE.	H.A.C. – 69 M.G.Cy
GUILLEMONT	17th March		The enemy retired without even firing a single shot and at about 11.0AM our men were to be seen walking about in No Man's Land. About 2.30 P.M. our front line advanced to a position on the BAPAUME – PERONNE ROAD when our MOON TRENCH at 4.0 P.M. Supports moved up to within about 50 yards our own side of the BAPAUME – PERONNE ROAD and our front line pushed on to about 100 yds other side of the road. At the front – a little sniping from the enemy was all the activity to be heard. Two of our M.G's were sent forward just behind our line. An enemy M.G. was in action in WIND MILL TRENCH enough and on our left in touch with 4TH AUSTRALIAN DIV: Front line	2/27 ABRAHAMS [con?t'd]

WAR DIARY or INTELLIGENCE SUMMARY

Army Form C. 2118.

Place	Date	Hour	Summary of Events and Information	Remarks and references to Appendices
GUILLEMONT	17th March 1917	contd	was then 150 yds in front of three guns, which in front 600 yds in front of that. VILLAGES OCCUPIED LE TRANSLOY. The remaining guns of this Coy were in its reserve. Casualties NIL. WEATHER FINE.	1 NCO + 59 MG Coy
GUILLEMONT	18th March		Since the enemy retirement yesterday the attack has been absolutely silent; about 9 to 10 A.M. the morning enemy fired about 12 shots somewhere into the back area. At 5.0 A.M. this morning ROEQUINEY was occupied by a patrol of 11 R.B. an afternoon patrol went through it. Afterwards our front was advanced to its extreme position of ROEQUINEY, other villages are known to have been occupied but no official intimation has been received. This Coy was relieved by 61 Coy all limbers and a half hour taken over. Offe reliefs Coy returned in marching order to BRIQUETTERIE. WEATHER FINE.	

WAR DIARY or INTELLIGENCE SUMMARY

Army Form C. 2118.

Place	Date	Hour	Summary of Events and Information	Remarks and references to Appendices
BRIQUETTERIE NEAR MONTAUBAN	19th March 1917		Coy resting and cleaning equipment. Casualties Nil. WEATHER DULL.	Ab 24 57 & 96
BRIQUETERIE	20th March 1917		Coy overhauling gas respirators, cleaning hut and ammunition. Casualties Nil. Coy paid in the afternoon. WEATHER WET.	
BRIQUETERIE	21st March		Coy training. Small arm drill etc. Spare parts & guns made up. Issue of personnel kit. Casualties - 1 O.R. admitted to Hosp. sick. WEATHER FINE	
BRIQUETERIE	22nd March		All officers and eight N.C.O's attended lecture on open fighting by Brig. Gen. Brown. Clayton of the Coliseum, Carnoy. Coy training. Coy drill etc. Casualties. Nil. 4 O.R. arrived from Base. WEATHER. FINE.	
BRIQUETERIE	23rd March		Coy training. Small arm drill etc. Casualties. Nil. WEATHER SNOW.	
BRIQUETERIE	24th March		O.O. received to relieve Co. M.G. Coy. in the line. Coy preparing for the line. Casualties. Nil. WEATHER. FINE.	

WAR DIARY or INTELLIGENCE SUMMARY

Army Form C. 2118.

Place	Date	Hour	Summary of Events and Information	Remarks and references to Appendices
BRIQUETERIE	25th March 1917		Coy left camp at BRIQUETERIE 11.30 A.M. and proceeded to HAIE WOOD where they had a hot dinner. They then proceeded to 60 M.G.Coy. H.Qrs at SAILLE-SAILLISEL where guides awaited them from each gun team. Relief was carried out in daylight and completed by 7.0 P.M. Twelve guns in the line had one section in reserve in dug-outs at HAIE WOOD. All limbers and hill down taken over. Enemy very quiet. Casualties. Nil.	#1 K.R. to 59 M.G Coy
SAILLE6M-SAILLISEL	26th March		At 12.0 midnight on night 26-25th the hind was put forward by one trench.	WEATHER. FINE.
			Coy in the line. Our covering patrols sent out villages which were on our right by Infantry. At 12.0 midnight 20th Division was to be relieved from the XIVth CORPS to the 7th Corps. Casualties. Nil.	WEATHER. WET.
SAILLE — SAILLISEL.	27th March.		On the night of the 26-27th inst. O.O. received to send 1 section of four gun forward to the following places :—	

Contd.

WAR DIARY or INTELLIGENCE SUMMARY

Army Form C. 2118.

Place	Date	Hour	Summary of Events and Information	Remarks and references to Appendices
SAILLY — SAILLESEL	27th March (1917)	CONTD	Two guns to BEET ROOT FACTORY with two platoons one gun to FOUR WINDS FARM with two platoons one gun to LEECES with two platoons. These guns were to be used to engage any enemy towns - and opposite range. They would to be fired upon they 6-0 A.M. This sector had to go a day round of 3½ miles on on every dark night. We gave in a enlargement of 30 mm from the 10th R.B. Casualties. NIL. WEATHER. WET.	NILCZ 69MGC691
SAILLY — SAILLESEL	28th March		Coy HeadQr moved to the Sunken road in MESNIL-EN-ARROUAISE also Coy transport lines moved from BRIQUETERIE to MESNIL-EN-ARROUAISE. Casualties. NIL. WEATHER. WET.	
MESNIL-EN-ARROUAISE	29th March		1 Section & 2 Officers of 217 Coy (Div: Coy) attached to us to-day. Two gun teams of No 4 Section and two of new Coy sent up the line to reserve positions under 2/Lt ABRAHAMS. Casualties. NIL. WEATHER. WET.	

WAR DIARY
or
INTELLIGENCE SUMMARY

Army Form C. 2118.

Place	Date	Hour	Summary of Events and Information	Remarks and references to Appendices
ESNES EN ARROUAISE	30th March 1917	night 29th/30th inst. 4-0 P.M.	O.O. received for an advance on the 30th commencing 4 P.M. Our guns were sited for advance planned by Bn not communicated. Front objective was Q32.c.0.0. running N.W. to Q.31. central. MAP.REF 57° S.E. All objectives P.30 central. P.23 central. Coy 15 dgrs moved to about taken with very few casualties. Bde also moved to nearby P.32 b.1.8 near CANAL STATION. On guns team under 2/Lt Wilson completely of CANAL STATION. buried, 2 men severe shell shock, two men slight shell shock. 1 O.R. wounded through the stomach. WEATHER. WET.	1/M.G.C. 59 M.G. Coy

2449 Wt. W14957/Mg0 750,000 1/16 J.B.C. & A. Forms/C.2118/12.

Vol 14

War Diary.

59th Machine Gun Company.

April 1917

WAR DIARY
or
INTELLIGENCE SUMMARY

(Erase heading not required.)

Army Form C. 2118.

Place	Date	Hour	Summary of Events and Information	Remarks and references to Appendices
CANAL STATION. P.32.B.18. MAP 57.C.SE.	31st March 1917.		Enemy quiet. Consolidation in progress in the line. Captured yesterday by us. No casualties. WEATHER FINE.	Made by S.T.M.C.Co.
"	1st April		Enemy fairly active with artillery. One man of 217 Coy (our Coy) killed by 77 m.m shell. WEATHER. DULL.	
"	2nd April		Enemy aircraft active during the morning. One enemy aeroplane dropped bombs on Coy Horse Lines in Darkays. 6 then bombed Bde Horses, killing and wounding 15 horses. This aeroplane was engaged by our Lewis gun and machine gun fire and came down M.L on enemy lines were driven down during the day. Casualties M.L. WEATHER. STORMY.	
"	3rd April		Enemy shelling in vicinity of Coy hqrs all day. Towards dusk enemy aeroplanes carry out an air recce engaged by machine gun fire. Two of these aircraft brought down. Still division of two of our observation balloons which were brought down.	Contd.

Place	Date	Hour	Summary of Events and Information	Remarks and references to Appendices
CANAL STATION F.32.b.1.8. MAP 51C S.E.	3rd April 1917	CONT'D	drawn in flames. One section of 217 Coy relieved by another section of 217 Coy. Casualties 1 O.R. admitted to hospital sick. WEATHER. FINE.	What for 59 M Coy 59 M Coy
"	4th April 1917		During the night 3rd/4th and O.O. of an advance received orders. Advance guards of the 8th Div. to advance its line so as to include GOUZEAUCOURT WOOD from about Q.22.c.11 thence Q.28.b.00.10. hold at Q.35.a.30.80 thence South eastwards. Advance guards of the XXth Div: is to carry out an held a METZ-EN-COUTURE until a defensive strength on the Spur about Q.27.a. 2nd Objective to capture enemy trench running from Q.19.c.30.95. to R.18.c.40.15. Two Vickers guns for escorting Batt: went forward under orders from O.C. Batts. Viz:- 10th K.R.R.C. 11th K.R.R.C. 11th R.B. ZERO HOUR: 2.P.M. All objectives taken. 8th Div: held up slightly on right - in a rear measure to capture GOUZEAUCOURT WOOD. Casualties in 59/M.F. 5 km cttd at 25.70. About 200 prisoners taken by CONT'D	

WAR DIARY
or
INTELLIGENCE SUMMARY

Army Form C. 2118.

Place	Date	Hour	Summary of Events and Information	Remarks and references to Appendices
CANAL STATION. P32 61.8. MAP 57c SE	4th April 1917		Contd — by us. No casualties in the Coy. In the evening the following wire was received "President Wilson before CONGRESS declared war on GERMANY. Vote not yet taken aaa Ends." WEATHER SNOW.	MC ht 59 MG Coy
	5th April		XXth Div. Commander sends the following wire to B.G.C. 59 INF. BDE. "DW: Commander gun company on the successful gun and all such equipment carried out at METZ & HAVRINCOURT WOOD to-day. Condition of climate was most arduous and enemy resistance stubborn. Operations reflect great credit on all concerned and show the fine spirit of all troops concerned in your advance guard." About 3 p.m. relief orders received for that night by 61 M.G. Coy. Owing to the large area of which our guns were, it was a most difficult relief. Relief completed by about 12.20 a.m. All tripods and belt boxes taken over. Contd. Division al.

Army Form C. 2118.

WAR DIARY
or
INTELLIGENCE SUMMARY
(Erase heading not required.)

Instructions regarding War Diaries and Intelligence Summaries are contained in F. S. Regs., Part II. and the Staff Manual respectively. Title Pages will be prepared in manuscript.

Place	Date	Hour	Summary of Events and Information	Remarks and references to Appendices
CANAL STATION P.32.b.1.8. MAP 57°S.E.	5th April 1917		CONT D. Divisional Section attached to us were sent back to their Coy Hqrs at LE TRANSLOY. On relief the Coy proceeded to billets in ROCQUINEY in cellars or broken down houses. One O.R. reinforcement from Base received. WEATHER. FINE	War Diary 5th Coy
ROCQUINEY	6th April		Coy resting. One O.R. admitted to Hospital sick on this day and one the day. WEATHER. SHOWERY.	
ROCQUINEY	7th April		Coy cleaning guns, tarpaulins, lent horses etc also cleaning equipment. WEATHER. DULL.	
ROCQUINEY	8th April		Coy attended Church Parade at Div. Hqrs. WEATHER. FINE.	
ROCQUINEY	9th April		Owing to bad weather Coy were confined to billets. Pte ROCQUINEY was killed by H.V. gun about 3 rounds fired. Win received from Div. Hqrs. American Minister at Berlin entering Peace at this morning Tuesday Presidents declaration declaring War on Germany by passing popular Cont D	

WAR DIARY
or
INTELLIGENCE SUMMARY

(Erase heading not required.)

Army Form C. 2118.

Place	Date	Hour	Summary of Events and Information	Remarks and references to Appendices
ROCQUIGNY	9th April 1917		Proposed not indulged with the regard to Pincheing - at noon to-day ad. men. to A. AMERICA furnacery dealing over. WEATHER SNOW	W/L t/- 59 M.G.Co.
ROCQUIGNY	10th April		Weather conditions still very bad. Coy. packing limber in the afternoon. WEATHER SNOW	
ROCQUIGNY	11th April		Orders now received to relieve 60 Coy. in the line. C.O. reconnoitred positions during afternoon. About 10 km. run received post having duty for 26 hours. During the daytime received from 52 Divisional fighting E. of ARRAS. total numbers of guns over in 11,000. 100 guns dated 132 guns) 170 machine guns and 60 Trench Mortars. WEATHER WET	
ROCQUIGNY	12th April		Coy. resting and preparing for the line. Seven reinforce- ments arrived from Base. WEATHER WET	
ROCQUIGNY	13th April		L/Cpl. O. STURSBERG. admitted to CORPS REST STATION. Coy moved off by section will section limber commencing at 2-30 P.M. CONTD	

WAR DIARY
or
INTELLIGENCE SUMMARY

Army Form C. 2118.

Place	Date	Hour	Summary of Events and Information	Remarks and references to Appendices
ROCQUIGNY	13th April 1917	3-30 P.M.	Contd. All arrangements hitherto unknown & taken over. Relief completed by 9-0 P.M. H.Qrs at YTRES. Coy transport – 54MGCoy Stores and all details also at YTRES. WEATHER. FINE.	Major 54MGCoy
YTRES	14th April		Coy H.Qrs ordered to move to RAOULCOURT by D.H.Q. Now complete by 2.30 P.M. Two O.R's slightly burnt owing to a fire in the line and admitted to hospital. 14 guns in the line is as over that 5 have S.A.A with each gun. WEATHER. FINE.	
UYAU RAOULCOURT.	15th April		After a fairly heavy bombardment the enemy attacked the Corps on our left this morning. The attack drove in on a front of about 6 miles between HERMIES and NOREUIL. We gained a footing in LAGNICOURT but was driven out by a counter attack leaving about 230 prisoners. Heavy losses were inflicted on the enemy. During the night 14/15th and 4 O.R. of the Coy wounded with shrapnel. WEATHER FINE.	

WAR DIARY or INTELLIGENCE SUMMARY

Army Form C. 2118.

Place	Date	Hour	Summary of Events and Information	Remarks and references to Appendices
RUYAULCOURT	16th April 1917		During the night 15/16th inst one section of 217 Coy reported him still in instructions to port 4 guns in the "BROWN LINE". During the day No 3 Section was withdrawn from BERTINCOURT and placed in "strong points" below HAVRINCOURT WOOD. No 4 Section now in reserve at Coy Headqrs. Lt. D. L. HOWARD. M.C. Intelligence Officer reported to Bde Headqrs and Bde Intelligence officer. A mine exploded same two-day at about 12-20 P.M. at P.11.b.c.9.4. and another at 1-30 P.M. at P.10.c.6.5. Both these mines completely blocked up the road. A hostile aeroplane brought down our observation balloons about FINS this afternoon at 4-0 P.M. Casualties: nil. Enemy artillery quiet. Casualties NIL. WEATHER. SHOWERY.	MMC Lr SM GCy
RUYAULCOURT.	17th April.		WEATHER. SNOW.	
RUYAULCOURT.	18th April.		Lo Lt Seaton returned two gun teams of No 1 Section and 2 gun teams of No 2 Section. 2/Lt. A. BRAHAMS and a 2/Lt. & have both one gun teams of No 4 Section. CASUALTIES. NIL. WEATHER. RAIN.	
RUYAULCOURT.	19th April.		Wire received from Q.H.Q. to the effect that the French in their successful attack on the AISNE had captured 19,000 prisoners and 100 guns amongst many M.G's Coy in this casualties Nil. WEATHER. RAIN.	

WAR DIARY or INTELLIGENCE SUMMARY

Army Form C. 2118.

Place	Date	Hour	Summary of Events and Information	Remarks and references to Appendices
RUYAULCOURT	20th April 1917		Enemy shelled HERMIES intermittently during the day. Steam engine went seen between 5 & 6 o'clock west of FLESQUIERES about K23 D 4 9. Casualties:- 1 OR admitted to hospital (sick). WEATHER. FINE	M.G. Lt 59 M.G. Coy
RUYAULCOURT	21st April		Enemy shelled canal trench on left of front line between 9 P.M. and 5.9's also many at night boundary of Bde between 9 & 11 am. Casualties:- 2 OR admitted to hospital (sick) WEATHER. WET.	
RUYAULCOURT	22nd April		Enemy aeroplanes very active all day. three aeroplanes were brought down as the result of air fights. two were enemy planes, the other unknown. they had many planes over them it fell in German lines the other in the ANZAC lines (on our right) Aeroplanes flew too high for machine gun fire. Our line was attacked at 8.0 P.M. the Ed following :- Q.11.C.00.90 - TRESCAULT. (inclusive) - road junction Q.4.C.50.70 - crossroads Q.3 & 20.15. road junction Q.3.0.40.10 - thence South-west to a point at about Q.2d.9.4. thence west to Q.2.C.5.8 - K.31 exclusive. All dispositions taken as before :- W.L. WEATHER FINE	

WAR DIARY
or
INTELLIGENCE SUMMARY.
(Erase heading not required.)

Army Form C. 2118.

Place	Date	Hour	Summary of Events and Information	Remarks and references to Appendices
RUYAULCOURT	23rd April 1917		Nothing to report. Casualties Nil. Weather FINE.	
RUYAULCOURT	24th April		HERMIES shelled by enemy about 10 AM and 9 PM. Situation quiet. Casualties Nil. Z.O.R. Seah —	
RUYAULCOURT	25th April		Weather FINE. Our enemy aeroplanes very active at great heights. An out of range of M.G. fire. Artly Relief completed by 6-0 PM. Our relief Coy took over. Others of 16 Sqdn in the line. Officers & WOs took over as usual. Casualties Nil.	
BERTINCOURT	26th April		Coy H.Qrs at BERTINCOURT. Casualties Nil. Weather FINE.	
BERTINCOURT	27th April		Three (3) O.R. reported for Duty, two as infantry and one medically unfit. 2/Lt T.M. DRAPER a/Capt'd to NTR.	

WAR DIARY
or
INTELLIGENCE SUMMARY.
(Erase heading not required.)

Army Form C. 2118.

Place	Date	Hour	Summary of Events and Information	Remarks and references to Appendices
BERTINCOURT	27th April 1917		CONTD. R.F.C. Major. 2/Lt. J.H.M'ION. reported from M.G. Base and taken on the strength vice 2/Lt. T.M. DRAPER. Casualties Nil. Coy. Baths. Weather. Fine.	
BERTINCOURT	28th April		Coy. have moved to YPRES. and all guns were withdrawn to that village. Casualties. Nil. WEATHER. FINE.	
YPRES.	29th April		Coy training for 1 hour in the morning. All ablutions at new Debus coved baths. Church parade at 11-15. A.M. Casualties. Nil. WEATHER. FINE.	

59 M G Coy
Vol 15

War Diary
May 1916
Sgt G.J. Company
59th M.G. Company

WAR DIARY
or
INTELLIGENCE SUMMARY.
(Erase heading not required.)

Army Form C. 2118.

Place	Date	Hour	Summary of Events and Information	Remarks and references to Appendices
YPRES.	30th March 1917 to 2nd May	Coy training	Casualties 2 O.Rs. Sick	All 29.4.17 6/51
YPRES.	3rd May		Coy left YPRES and proceeded to relieve 60th M.G. Coy in the By night sector of Brim road front viz: front line Q.3.b.22. Q.4. central Q.5.a.O.1. map 57c N.E. Eight guns on this line, 4 guns in reserve lines and 4 about 3000x behind them. Two sections 1 (eight guns total) taking up positions in tubular shelter in HETZ. ENCOUTURE. The eight former in tubular shelter. Gun crews almost proceed forward would dumps. First commander took up their guns and rations to their gun positions. To avoid fatigue of handing our loading our ammo belt holes (in the case 16 Lewis and 1.4.5 belt boxes) were carried over. Relief completed with no casualties. About 10-0 P.M. STROMBOS horn sounded from the left. We immediately blew own 60th MG. Bets.	

WAR DIARY
INTELLIGENCE SUMMARY

Place	Date	Hour	Summary of Events and Information	Remarks and references to Appendices
YPRES	3rd May 1917		CONTD. Boll rung up to say that the 7th Somerset T.L. of 61st Inf. Bde had sent up the Gas S.O.S. The enemy had been shelling with gas shells which burst in the air and gave a curious red light lasting about 10 seconds. Wind was very strong and blowing towards our lines. About 10-30 P.M. Gas S.O.S was cancelled. Coy. H.Q.R. at a point shown on map. MAP.ref. P.29.a.3.7. MAP. 57c.NE. WEATHER FINE. I.O.R. admitted to hospital. Sick.	Note 59h,f,coy
P.29.a.3.7	4th May		Coy in the line as above. Another false gas alarm was given on the night of 4th/5th. The reason given was that the enemy were throwing up rockets which burn + eventually the same as the rockets used by us for gas attack. Casualties. Nil. WEATHER FINE.	
P.29.a.3.7.	5th May to 7th May		Coy in the line. Casualties. 1.O.R. admitted to hospital. Sick. WEATHER FINE.	

Army Form C. 2118.

WAR DIARY
or
INTELLIGENCE SUMMARY.
(Erase heading not required.)

WWL L —
59th M.G.Coy.

Place	Date	Hour	Summary of Events and Information	Remarks and references to Appendices
P.29.a.3.7.	May 8th 1917		The following new emplacements dug in position in	
MAP.57cNE			front line: Q.11.b.2.8. to join S.E. Q.5.a.0.0. to join N.E. Q.4.a.80.05 to join N.W. Q.4.a.00.20 to join N.W.	MAP. 57c NE.
	May 9th		A new position in reserve trench dug at Q.10.b.0.5. to join N.E. The above position was syplied to infantry on ground. Counterattack. N.W. 2.0.R. connected from Bane.	WEATHER FINE.
P.29.a.3.7.	May 9th	10th	At 10 P.M. on the night 9/9th the Divn. ictl. Commander sent for the four M.G. Coy Commanders & told Division was again to. attack enemy's strong point on the HINDENBURG LINE to commence at 2 P.M. and from to at 2-15 P.M. the object was to make the enemy show his observation balloon which our aeroplanes were then to bomb. A very desultory artillery fire also helped in. The enemy started no balloons. 8 of our M.G.s returned about Q.3.c.5.0. (4 guns) and Q.9.a.5.4. (4 guns) fired about 20,000 rounds. The above scheme was carried out on the entire 4th Army Front. ONE.	

Lon Pol.

WAR DIARY
or
INTELLIGENCE SUMMARY.

(Erase heading not required.)

Army Form C. 2118.

Abb. W=

Place	Date	Hour	Summary of Events and Information	Remarks and references to Appendices
P.29.a.3.7 Map. 57°N.E.	May 11th 1917	10ᴬ	Contᵈ One of our aircraft brought news in pieces by two enemy planes. The pilot dropped about 300ˣ from METZ-EN-COUTURE. Coy edge moved to the edge of HAVRIN-COURT WOOD about @ P.9.d.5.8. Casualties NIL. WEATHER. FINE.	MAP 57°N.E.
HAVRINCOURT WOOD.	May 11th.		Nothing to report. Casualties. 2 O.R. admitted to hospital sick. 1 O.R. reported from hospital. WEATHER. FINE.	
HAVRINCOURT WOOD.	May 12th		Enemy aircraft were fairly active all day. The Coy. guns are now in 4 guns in front line, 4 guns in reserve line, 4 guns on edge of wood, 4 guns in reserve at Coy H.Qrs. Casualties nil. WEATHER. FINE.	
HAVRINCOURT WOOD.	May 13th		On the night of the 13th/14th the Divn. co-operated in the enemy's raiding about 90ˣ. In consequence of which two guns were taken over from 60 M.G. Coy. Casualties NIL. WEATHER. FINE.	

Army Form C. 2118.

WAR DIARY
or
INTELLIGENCE SUMMARY.
(Erase heading not required.)

WD of 59 M.G. Coy.

Place	Date	Hour	Summary of Events and Information	Remarks and references to Appendices
HAVRINCOURT WOOD	May 14th 1917		2 O.R. wounded indirect fire area K.34.d. from 12 midnight to 1 A.M. and 3 A.M. to 6 A.M. 7 m.g. ain aft Theodolite aug. to be compared to night. 9.16 a. 3.3 to fire at enemy hows Battery and Q.11.d. 4.5. C.S. to fire down valley towards DOAR COPSE. During night 13/14/17 that area a very heavy storm. Visibility NIL. WEATHER FINE.	MAP 57c NE.
HAVRINCOURT WOOD	May 15th		2 guns did indirect fire between 11.0pm & 12 mn + 3.0am to 4.0am on HINDENBURG LINE made infront of K.35.f. + 1700 rds between 12 mn & 10 am. also 3.0 am to 4.0 am on crater at X roads K.36.c.0.1 from an Q.6.d. At 2.0 am indirect fire was returned to be harassing patrols &c. Sgt overseer reports that he ceased fire at 1.0 am. M.G. on left were doing indirect fire all night. This diaries accounts for the inform. The 2 new emplacements (see above) have been occupied.	Col. L. 57NE7

WAR DIARY
or
INTELLIGENCE SUMMARY.

Army Form C. 2118.

Col. h.

Place	Date	Hour	Summary of Events and Information	Remarks and references to Appendices
AVRINCOURT WOOD	MAY 16th		4000 rounds Indirect fire during the night on K35 b.1.c. Reamers unknown.	MAP 57c N.E.
			Enemy artillery slacking off.	
RIENCOURT WOOD	MAY 17th		Indirect fire : nil.	
			Hostile Indirect fire into PRESCOURT at 8.0pm.	
AVRINCOURT WOOD	MAY 18th		1000 rounds Indirect fire from 12mn. to 1.0am on X roads K36C.0.1.	
			Enemy artillery more active. In the evening several 5.9s fell near forward guns. No casualties.	
AVRINCOURT WOOD	MAY 19th		500 rounds Indirect fire from 10pm to 11.45pm on K35 c.r.d.	Col. h. 57 N.E.
			British aeroplane brought down in flames by enemy plane at about 4.30pm fell behind our lines N.E. of MŒUVRES-EN-COUTURE.	
			2Lt MARTIN 176 proceeded on leave to commence 21st May.	

WAR DIARY
or
INTELLIGENCE SUMMARY.
(Erase heading not required.)

Army Form C. 2118.

Co. Hr.

Place	Date	Hour	Summary of Events and Information	Remarks and references to Appendices
ARMENTIERES WOOD	May 20th		Weather fine: NIL. Enemy aeroplane brought down by L/Cpl JOHNSTONE (No 3 Sec under 2LT LANE) at 11.45 a.m. falling behind FRONT LINE in Q.16 whilst A/A Artillery were all firing at the aeroplane. L/Cpl JOHNSTONE fired a burst at it, the plane passed over the gun position being well behind the FRONT LINE. The M.G. continued firing til plane landed behind the FRONT LINE. The pilot was badly wounded in the leg, the wounds having been caused by bullets fired afterwards from behind him. This disposes of the claim by two Lewis gunners who firing up the plane from the FRONT LINE, claim that they brought it down. Before was made an inc. to Pde, who were satisfied that it was my gun which brought the plane down. 1 O.R. admitted to hospital sick. Advance party of 126th M.G. Coy arrived, the which Coy is to relieve us tomorrow night. 3 offrs + 12 O.R.s went into line for the night.	Ch.S/ Lr 57 Mcg

WAR DIARY
or
INTELLIGENCE SUMMARY.
(Erase heading not required.)

Army Form C. 2118.

Vol 6

Place	Date	Hour	Summary of Events and Information	Remarks and references to Appendices
NEUVILLE BOURJONVAL	May 21st		Relieved by 126 Infantry. Night spent in billets in NEUVILLE BOURJONVAL.	
E TRANSLOY	May 22nd		Proceeded at 9.0 a.m. to billets in LE TRANSLOY. Night spent here.	
BARREUR	May 23rd		Proceeded at 9.30 a.m. to BARREUR. Lectures dec 1+2 went straight into the lines to relieve the 2 Forward Sections of 5th AUST. M.G.Coy. Rest of Coys. to C.23.9.0. where 1 O.R. admitted to hospital sick.	
C.22.d.6.4.	MAY 24th		Completed relief of other two Coys. Dispositions: 2 guns in forward position + " in Reserve line + " in Coys in Coys.9.0. C.22.d.6.4. with 3 anti-aircraft M reserve guns. 3250 rounds fired on enemy showing during discharge of gas at 2.0 a.m. heavy enemy shelling followed during the following	Map. 57cN1 C23.d 57c/1/2/3

WAR DIARY
or
INTELLIGENCE SUMMARY.
(Erase heading not required.)

Army Form C. 2118.

a/b 57 M.G. Coy

Place	Date	Hour	Summary of Events and Information	Remarks and references to Appendices
			Casualties. Cpl KYNE (wounded)	
			Ptes BRACE + OWEN (shell shock)	
C22d 6.A.	May 25th to 27th		Coy in line as previously stated. Shelling heavier than in HAVRINCOURT Sector. Thor. Right guns + Coy f. line guns heavily shelled on several occasions but no casualties occurred. Sounds fired on average by M. Coy.	
BEAUCAMPE	May 28th		Coy relieved by M.Coy. About 6.0 p.m. Coy Hqrs heavily shelled with 5.9 (percussion + shrapnel). No casualties. Coy marched to billets at BEAUCAMPE ; H.18.a.	Odf M 57MG
BEAUCAMPE	May 29th	9.30	1 O.R. to hospital sick. Coy training.	

WAR DIARY OF 59th Coy. MGC

JUNE 1917.

WAR DIARY or INTELLIGENCE SUMMARY

Army Form C. 2118.

59 M.G.Coy
Cav. Bn.

Place	Date	Hour	Summary of Events and Information	Remarks and references to Appendices
BEUGNATRE	1917 31st May		Coy in rest billets. 1 O.R. to hospital sick. (training) Football.	
	1st June		Coy in rest billets. 1 O.R. ditto. ditto	
	2nd		ditto	
	3rd		By sports (under 59 T.M.B.) in afternoon. During fly of war, one of our aeroplanes (under 59 T.M.B.) on afternoon. During fly of the enemy's cavalry 1 O.R. wounded, with seven to fracture, in the middle of (of 59 T.M.B.) also wounded (severe concussion + normal pass vintage). Both went to H.A.C. Under to Improving brewing station	
	4th		Training. All too inefficient. Improved by Bn. Geo. Offr. Another ditto. All ranks instructed by Bde. Bombing Offr. to use of live bombs.	
	5th		Relieved 108 M.G. Coy in left sector. 3 atn. 2 m.g.'s front line under 12d & 16 of Bullecourt ("Right at C21 C117 (guns in front + Support lines to on Reserve line. 3.4 on reserve.	

B.R.

WAR DIARY
or
INTELLIGENCE SUMMARY.
(Erase heading not required.)

Army Form C. 2118.

Place	Date	Hour	Summary of Events and Information	Remarks and references to Appendices
NOREUIL	7-6-17		Coy in line. Enemy artillery active. Casualties nil. WEATHER FINE.	
NOREUIL	8-6-17		One gun and tripod in the C/P M Brigade Sector destroyed by enemy trench mortars. Casualties. one shell shock. Intermittent shelling of front line also trench mortars all day. WEATHER FINE.	
NOREUIL	9-6-17		Nothing to report.	
NOREUIL	10-6-17 to 10th inst.		Capt. S.E. ODGERS returned from Egypt. Coming on S. side of the pillars. The enemy artillery have been extremely quiet - latterly. On the night of the 13/14 inst. ents - section of relief took place. Casualties Nil. WEATHER FINE.	
NOREUIL	15-6-17			
NOREUIL	15-6-17		Lieut. H.H. Cassidy (Second in command) proceeds to UK as applicant for transfer to Indian Army. Lieut. A.M. Cameron reports on being posted to the Company. Shown down for 3 officers are ment out to Railway Employment Coy. as being surplus for company Establishment.	

T2134. Wt. W708-776. 500000. 4/16. Str J. C. & S.

WAR DIARY or INTELLIGENCE SUMMARY

Army Form C. 2118.

Place	Date	Hour	Summary of Events and Information	Remarks and references to Appendices
NOREUIL	15.6.17		Three guns fired intermittently throughout the night on western approaches to Riencourt. Enemy had a number of M.G. bursts on new support trench, apparently ranging. Barrage. Our O.R. wounded self inflicted. Weather fine.	
NOREUIL	16.6.17		Situation fairly quiet. One O.R. admitted to hospital. Weather fine.	
NOREUIL	17.6.17		Indirect fire (M.G. cmd) carried on Riencourt by guns in reserve railway embankment. Result unknown. Alternative positions under construction for all front line guns. New emplacement contacted in sunken railway embankment. Enemy seems normal. In the light of summer dawn seen up during the night trepass a lorry train at 10.30 p.m. — at 2300 train 10 trucks and 2 am to night sweeping apparently reported on attack. One O.R. admitted to hospital. Weather fine.	
NOREUIL	18.6.17		Guns in emplacement fire indirect on Riencourt. Bullecourt. NM. Weather fine.	
NOREUIL	19.6.17		Patrol fire carried out upon Bruno road junction. O/R raid relieving our guns recent to relieve artillery activity. All normal. Canadian NM.	
NOREUIL	20.6.17		6 guns (2 each from Coy HQ) registered targets during wish on enemy trenches with indirect fire from Rocher. On advice of O.C. 10th Bn. K.R.R. the registrations was carried out firing several rounds per minute.	

T2134. Wt. W708—776. 500000. 4/16. Sir J. C. & S.

WAR DIARY
or
INTELLIGENCE SUMMARY.
(Erase heading not required.)

Army Form C. 2118.

Place	Date	Hour	Summary of Events and Information	Remarks and references to Appendices
NOEUX	21.6.17.		so as to deceive the enemy giving the impression of relief & not of barrage. Result: fire unknown. Ammunition expended 9000 rounds. The Lt Pa gun was then withdrawn to Coy H.Q. Enemy shelled right front line - C.T. with us & a shell sunk. 10.0 P.M. midnight. Casualties: One OR killed, 3 OR's wounded (3 seriously) by shell fire. Weather Rainy. from S.O.P.H onwards. 6.15 M.G.C. began relief 10.30 P.M. Relief complete 2.0 A.M. Casualties 1 OR killed.	MAP 57c 2nd Lt Mc 3rd course
GOMIECOURT	22.6.17.		1 wounded (drill wing), 1 shell shock. Weather Rainy. Enemy shelling at intervals. Coy in Reserve Billets near Killers, BEUGNATRE. 1 OR to hospital sick.	
BEUGNATRE	23.6.17.		Commenced overhauling kit, prior to move to reorganization & recuperation course.	
GOMIECOURT	24.6.17.		Proceeded to GOMIECOURT taking over at 10.17 Camp from 212 M.Coy. Billets at FAVREUIL. Handed over to M.Coy.	
GOMIECOURT	25.6.17.		Deficiencies of clothing & equipments completed.	
GOMIECOURT	26.6.17.		Deficiencies of gun stores & spare parts drawn fixed.	
GOMIECOURT	27.6.17. 28.6.17.		Musketry training & preparation for move on 29th. 2Lt LANE & 13 OR's returned from course on 25th. 1 OR to hospital sick on that date.	
SPRELLE LES DOUARS	29.6.17.		Remained at ACHIET LE GRAND demanded at CANDAS marched to F.Arnst with Total Strength in command Lt. Col. Bromley, Major Amos, & 20 Others, 132 OR's 12 Lewis guns, 2 pack	not in course reorganism

Vol 17

War Diary
50th Machine Gun Coy.
July 1917

WAR DIARY
or
INTELLIGENCE SUMMARY.   59 M.G. Coy.

Army Form C. 2118.

Place	Date	Hour	Summary of Events and Information	Remarks and references to Appendices
St LEGER LES-DOMART	29.6.17		Entrained at ACHEUX-LE-GRAND, detrained at ACHEUX. Proceeded on CANTONS marched to billets in ST LEGER-LES-DOMART	MAP 57C.
St LEGER	30.6.17		Engineering started, in accordance with a training Programme drawn 30.6.17.	
St LEGER	1.7.17			
St LEGER	2.7.17		Eng training continued. 1 OR to hospital sick.	
St LEGER	3.7.17		ditto Lt MacGILLIVRAY returned from Course at CAMIERS	
St LEGER	4.7.17		ditto 2nd Lt Garner joined.	
St LEGER	5.7.17		Capt Burgess by G.O.C. 2nd Divn. at 12 noon near BERTRANCOURT. 1 OR to hospital sick.	O.o.l.
St LEGER	6.7.17		Eng training continued. NCOs special class under Brigade Physical Training Instructor.	
St LEGER	7.7.17		Eng training continued. 3 OR to hospital sick.	
St LEGER	8.7.17		Company Church Parade.	
St LEGER	9.7.17		Company training continued. 1 OR to hospital.	
St LEGER	10.7.17		Company training ditto.	
St LEGER	11.7.17		ditto Brigade sports in aft.	
St LEGER	12.7.17		- ditto - 1 OR to hospital sick	
St LEGER	13.7.17		- ditto -	
St LEGER	14.7.17		- ditto -	
St LEGER	15.7.17		Coy having Church Parade. 1 OR to hospital.	a.m.e.

Army Form C. 2118.

WAR DIARY
or
INTELLIGENCE SUMMARY.
(Erase heading not required.)

Instructions regarding War Diaries and Intelligence Summaries are contained in F. S. Regs., Part II. and the Staff Manual respectively. Title pages will be prepared in manuscript.

Place	Date	Hour	Summary of Events and Information	Remarks and references to Appendices
ST LEGER	16.7.17		Company training in accordance with Intensive training programme	
ST LEGER	17.7.17		– ditto – 1 Officer to hospital sick.	
ST LEGER	18.7.17		– ditto –	
ST LEGER	19.7.17		– ditto – OC Coy proceeded on courses	Sheet 27 F.15 BRE.
ST LEGER	20.7.17		Entrained at Fusvillers Canadian station with transport. Detrained at Pernes & marched to billets at Cornolles	
CANADA	21.7.17		Company inspected by C.O. Rifle exercises & drill	
CANADA	22.7.17		Church Parade for C of E + R.C.S. 1 O.R. attached wounded during air raid	
CANADA	23.7.17		Company of 54th Ches bhy & Transport moved to Bryan Camp at Lozinghem	A16 a 6.6.
DRAGON CAMP	24.7.17		Physical Drill. Cleaned guns, bayonets, gas helmets & picked limbers. OC Coy & Section Officers practised rifle & unsheltered positions. 9 pm Lectures Officers numbers battens practised to positions in 12 hours. S.A.A. cart sets up. Bayonets practised to "Bayonet Fighting" pts improvements + drug yrs. 3 comp each left & Coy agreement win. 1 O.R (attached) admitted to hospital sick. 0700 – 1 O.R wounded Shrapnel.	
DRAGON CAMP	25.7.17		Rifle, + inspection of feet. Ammunition in belts cleaned + dried Sentries in the line relieved. Physical Training + inspection	
DRAGON CAMP	26.7.17		Rifle exercises. 1 O.R admitted to hospital.	

WAR DIARY
or
INTELLIGENCE SUMMARY

Army Form C. 2118.

Place	Date	Hour	Summary of Events and Information	Remarks and references to Appendices
DRAGOON CAMP.	27.7.17		Physical Training. All ranks of M.G's inspected D.A.D.o.S. 20th Bde. 2/Lt. Bodle to take up position in line to open fire at 5 p.m. O.R. 3 killed & 8 wounded.	
"	28.7.17		Boche counter attack. We got 16 guns firing in S.O.S lines put in front of Infantry. Fired 83 belts. 20,450 rounds. 1 O.R. admitted to hospital sick (attached).	
"	29.7.17		Rounds fired about 5000. Casualties 2 O.R. wounded. Still fair. Slight. 1 O.R. gassed. Heavy shelling all round position. Sgt Farnham to 146 M.G.Coy on promotion to C.S.M.	
"	30.7.17		Company at its in line. No casualties — Rounds fired 5000. Total strength begins of month 11 Officers 194 O.R. Includes attached. End of month 12 Officers 226 O.R. Includes attached. " Casualties killed, wounded, sick 1 Officer 20 O.R. Drafts received 15 O.R. Another joined returned 6 O.R.	

A.M. Crompton Lt.

WAR DIARY
or
INTELLIGENCE SUMMARY.
(Erase heading not required.)

Army Form C. 2118.

JHM^cGy   JH/18

Place	Date	Hour	Summary of Events and Information	Remarks and references to Appendices
DRAGON CAMP	31.7.17	3.50 a.m.	Barrage of 85,000 rounds from 16 M. Guns. Company relieved from guns at noon to Rear H.Q. No casualties.	A 16 A.S.S.
"	1.8.17		Company rested. Weather did not permit a parade.	
"	2.8.17		Guns overhauled cleaned and deficiencies made good.	
"	3.8.17		All amm. cleaned. Guns limbers repaired.	
"	4.8.17		Inspection. Weather bad. Parade abandoned. C.O. on leave.	
"	5.8.17		Church Parade for all.	
"	6.8.17		Deficiencies of guns and clothing made up. Containers fixed on Box Respirators. (Instructions for attached men. D.M.G.O. and 2nd. in Command reconnoitred gun positions about C.3.d.8.8. (Sheet 28 N.W. 2)	
"	7.8.17		2nd. in Command & Section Officers recce gun positions about C.3.a.7.6 (Sheet 28 N.W.2). Chase + marked 16 emplacements. 16 Pack mules with 2 troops S.A.A. each sent up + amm. dumped about C 7 d.2.3.	
"	8.8.17		Limbers cleaned. Instruction for attached men. 1 O.R. to hospital. Ammunition taken by limbers to C8 a.7.7. and dumped.	
"	9.8.17		Box Respirator Drill. Belts filled, including 160 locks each to troops – these we packed into S.A.A. boxes. 32 troops S.A.A. taken by 16 mules driven + attached men to C7 d.2.3. In the evening a wiring party of 8 men and one Sgt. per section prepared the ground and made emplacements in shell holes.	CO Th

WAR DIARY or INTELLIGENCE SUMMARY

Army Form C. 2118.

59 M.G. Coy

Place	Date	Hour	Summary of Events and Information	Remarks and references to Appendices
DRAGON CAMP	10/8/17		Gun cleaned. Company Inspected. 2 OR to hospital, 7 to officers.	A.16 & 58.
"	11/8/17		Lieut Howitt returned from reinforcement camp & saw took his place. Lieut Hargreaves reported from Hot Cross.	
"	12/8/17		32 OR's SAA team firing. E7a.2.5 to gun position. by Scott Him with gun & classes. Church Parade. Bomb Practice. 2 OR to hospital. 2 returned. Shell fire. 12 shell bore T & SAA bore returned to path hills and then to gun position from dump at C8 a 7.7. 4 mules wounded on the way.	
"	13/8/17		Barrage practice. Sgt Major & 2 OR wounded by high shell shell at rest in the camp. Remainder of Amm taken forward from dump — L/C Thompson carrying ordinance of C.S.M. 1 OR. 1 mule wounded at Advanced Transport Lines, Brielen.	
"	14/8/17		Coy (less transport) moved to MALAKOFF FARM CAMP. All sections laid out harrass lines & proceeded to barrage emplacements (7 hours SAA) to each emplacement returning for amm. (12 belt boxes & 7 boxes SAA) — all firing during Night. 5 OR (2 attd) wounded — all firing during to camp at dawn. 14/15 Alright. Marched up after dark firing, prepared positions, Coy HQrs at artillery OP. C3.a.45.45. for 1-2 Secs on a line from C3a 35.95 to U7c 20.20 hr. Nos 3 & 4 Secs on a line from	MAP LINKENHOEK 1:10000
"	15.8.17			

WAR DIARY
or
INTELLIGENCE SUMMARY

Army Form C. 2118.

59 M.G.Coy

Place	Date	Hour	Summary of Events and Information	Remarks and references to Appendices
ALANOFF FARM	15.8.17 Contd.		Barrage lines: 1+2 Secs (i) Reserve trench in U23a, lifting to (ii) track in U17. 3+4 Secs (i) Road U22d.9.2 to U22d.35.95 lifting to (ii) Road U23.20.15 to U23.40.90.	
"	16.8.17		Zero hour 4.30 a.m. Heavy hostile barrage was opened about dawn of STEENBECK, which continued with the same intensity throughout the battle. From 4.30 am - 5.30 am a barrage of 4 secs was laid on Nos 3+4 secs positions. From 2 to 2+10 minutes Nos 3+4 secs fired on (i) target, + from 2+10 to 2+60 minutes fired on (ii) target. Nos 1+2 secs fired from 2+10 to 2+150 secs on (i) + from 2+150 to 2+195 on (ii). During the battle, 2/Lt Moon (i/c No 1 Sec) was wounded + proceeded to dressing station. 2/Lt Wilson (i/c No 2 Sec) was also wounded, but assumed command of No 1 Sec as well + continued in command of the 8 guns until the Coy was relieved. Excellent work was done by him, by L/Cpl TROTTER (No 1 Sec) + L/Cpl HAWKES (No 2 Sec). Cpt COFY MGCRs also set a fine example, staying with the guns	

WAR DIARY
INTELLIGENCE SUMMARY

59 M.G.Cg Title pages

Army Form C. 2118.

Place	Date	Hour	Summary of Events and Information	Remarks and references to Appendices
IMAROTZ FARM	16.8.17	Noon	During the time they were firing & generally encouraging everyone by his manner. After the cessation of our artillery barrage, the fire of Nos 1 & 2 Secs remained on their barrage lines as S.O.S. guns & those of Nos 3 Sec were mounted for anti-aircraft work. Casualties: KILLED: 3 ORs. WOUNDED: 2 OFFRS. (2Lts Nelson & Mony) 19 ORs (5 attd.) About 90 rpp Rounds fired. In the afternoon, an order was received to lend 1 Sec to reinforce Divl flank, to report to C.O. 89 when they were at ALOUETTE FARM. Before No a Sec (Lt Stubbs) had moved off, the order was cancelled.	
"	17.8.17		Coy remained in previous position. About 20 rounds S.A.A. were fired on hostile aircraft. 1 O.R. killed & 3 O.R. wounded. Ot. 1113 Coy called onw Lg ster & agreed to take	Coph.

WAR DIARY
INTELLIGENCE SUMMARY

Army Form C. 2118.

59/M.G.Coy

Place	Date	Hour	Summary of Events and Information	Remarks and references to Appendices
MAAMOUF FARM.	17.8.17	6 p.m.	over huts, S.A.A. & Genl bins.	
"	18.8.17		About 1.0 a.m. direct hit on ammn. Lorry by H.E. 4.2 exploding about 25 Mills Bombs & a dozen or so rounds S.A.A. setting light to 8 Smk Verey lights. Orders received through 60 Bde H.Q. at 10.30 a.m. (STRAY FARM) to evacuate position venue to MAAMOUF FARM. Guns limbered their implementa (Kear belt boxes & S.A.A. left to be taken over) were carried down by gun teams to daylight dump & were removed thence by transport. Coy entrained at EL VICTARDINGATE at 8.15 p.m., detrained at PROVEN & marched to occupy previous camp. 1 O.R. wounded. 2 O.R. wounded as reinforcements.	

Army Form C. 2118.

WAR DIARY
or
INTELLIGENCE SUMMARY.
(Erase heading not required.)

59/M G. Coy

Place	Date	Hour	Summary of Events and Information	Remarks and references to Appendices
PROVEN	19.8.17.		Coy cleaned up & made up practically all deficiencies from salved guns & spare parts lovers brought out of the line.	
"	20.8.17.		CAPT ROGERS proceeded on leave to U.K. Coy training with particular attention to Barrage fire, drill with Lyser striped Shuffage. 2 LT WATT reported for duty. 4 O.R. arrived as reinforcements.	
"	21.8.17.		LT MOGG proceeded on leave to U.K. Coy training. 8 O.R. arrived as reinforcements.	
"	22.8.17.		ditto. 1 O.R. arrived as reinforcement. 1 O.R. leave to U.K.	
"	23.8.17.		ditto. 1 O.R. (attd) to hospital sick. 1 O.R. leave to U.K.	
"	24.8.17.		ditto. 1 O.R. (attd) to hospital sick.	
"	25.8.17.		ditto.	
"	26.8.17.		ditto. 2 LT PAGE & CAPT joined Coy. 1 O.R. (attd) to hospital sick. 1 O.R. leave to U.K.	
"	27.8.17.		ditto. 1 O.R. (attd) to hospital sick. 2 O.R. leave to U.K.	
"	28.8.17.		LT MACGILLIVRAY proceeded on leave to U.K. 2 O.R. to U.K. on leave.	
"	29.8.17.		Coy training. 2 LT WILSON to CCS (septic poisoning from wound).	AHM
"	30.8.17.		ditto.	

WAR DIARY
or
INTELLIGENCE SUMMARY

Army Form C. 2118.

59 M.G.Coy

Place	Date	Hour	Summary of Events and Information		Remarks and references to Appendices
Aug 1917				Off. O.R.	
			Strength at beginning of month	11	168
			ditto end of month	11	176
			Total Casualties			
			Killed & wounded	2	36 (including 9 attd)
			Sick	1	12
			Drafts received	2	32
			from hospital		7

[signature]

Army Form C. 2118.

WAR DIARY
or
INTELLIGENCE SUMMARY.

(Erase heading not required.)

59 MGC

Vol 19

Instructions regarding War Diaries and Intelligence Summaries are contained in F. S. Regs., Part II. and the Staff Manual respectively. Title pages will be prepared in manuscript.

Place	Date	Hour	Summary of Events and Information	Remarks and references to Appendices
HUCH CAMP	31.8.17		Company Training, including Physical drill.	F.15.b.6.8 Sheet 29
"	1.9.17		Firing MG guns on 25 yds range. all 4 & attached men as well.	
"	2.9.17		Church parade for all.	
"	3.9.17		Company Training, including P.T. & Company drill. Guns cleaned.	
"	4.9.17		" " " " Gun drill	
"	5.9.17		Supplied working parties for R.E.s. Baths for all. 26 Rts to hospital.	
"	6.9.17		2nd in Com'd attended cooking demonstration. 50 in the month, 20 in aft.	
"	7.9.17		Supplied working parties for R.E.s. " " " "	
"	8.9.17		" " " " " " " "	
"			2 O.R. admitted to hospital.	
Dunbar	9.9.17		Company including Transport moved forward 8 guns relieved No 115 M.G. Coy at 29 A.6. T & guns at U.28.D.9.9.	B.20.a.5.4 Sheet 28
"			Coy HQ V.27.c.4.5. Took over 8 huts for guns, 3 huts for gun.	
"	10.9.17		1 O.R. wounded slightly at hand. Run under of day at Bn HQ. P.T.T	
			drivers cleaned. Heavy shelling, what by Seton Offeress. no casualties.	
"	11.9.17		Remainder P.T. Foot fatigue.	

WAR DIARY or INTELLIGENCE SUMMARY

Army Form C. 2118.

Place	Date	Hour	Summary of Events and Information	Remarks and references to Appendices
Zuudiph	12.9.17		No 4 Section withdrawn to Bn HQ. No casualties	B20 a.54 Sheet 28
	13.9.17		Shelling continues. 1 O.R. man admitted hospital.	
	14.9.17		Remainder P.T. Company fatigues.	
	15.9.17		No thing of importance to report. Gunner died in SOS bring him in from No 3 Section, was relieved by men of this an section	
	16.9.17		No 2 section relieved No 3 section, died a night SOS firing. 1 O.R. to hospital.	
			No 3 Section returned to advanced HQ.	
	19.9.17		Nothing of importance to report. 8 guns in hand. SOS	
			1 O.R. to hospital. 2 in H.Q + No 3 Section - mounted from HQ. U 29. A + 9.	
			No 3 Section 1 gun V 29. a + 0. 99. 1 gun in ruined cot at Bn HQ. 1 gun position in	
			cemetery tomb. 1 gun in position V 23. C 50. 60.	
			2 guns No 4 Section Shield. 2 O.R. wounded. Gun blown up. afterwards salvaged.	B22 b5.2.
indaff	18.9.17		Tamba post moved to CARDOEN FARM AREA. Rear HQ to B22 b 2.2. heavy shelling	
	19.9.17		1 O.R. wounded. 6 hundred guns moved up to assembly trench, link work up this	
Franch	20.9.17		2 guns under 2nd D A Maurand advanced to battered wood.	
			position about 80 yds to left of Rly line c 95. 15. Casualties killed 3 wounded.	
			2 guns under Sgt. Bayford mule held up when advancing. this officer	
			was put out of action the carried on from his position attacked by 4	
			wounded Huns & saw that they were returned safely.	
			This section fired about 5000 rounds	

WAR DIARY or INTELLIGENCE SUMMARY

Army Form C. 2118.

Place	Date	Hour	Summary of Events and Information	Remarks and references to Appendices
Malakoff Farm	20.9.17		Owing to the failure of the attack carried out by the 11th KRRC, his 3 Section field to withdraw to Cement Tunnel. 2nd Lt E.G. Watts was advised to withdraw. His unit in attack succeeded a single Tues Afgan posn. During these operations the gun engaged a hostile MG located U23 b 90.20. This section fired approx 3000 rounds. Total casualties this Section – 1 Officer (Sm burn) wounded. 2 O R killed. 12 O R wounded. During this operation Corp. Gardner kept his gun firing under intense bombardment.	Brown took shelter. B22 b 2 (Rear H.Q.)
"	21.9.17		This Section moved from Bay HQ at Malakan Enemies to U.23 c 5.60. No 2 " at Bay 11 B. No 3 " 29 guns to Rotten Row + 2 guns under By Billy forwarding the night of the Reg – No 4 " withdrew 1 gun to Cemetery trench. All guns continued to fire on position.	
"	22.9.17 23.9.17		No 1 Section withdrew + took on Bay 61 Bay at dawn. U28 a 20.50. No 2 Sect in bomb from By HQ + took up posn – in same line with No1 Section. No 3 Section withdrew + took posn – No 4 Section to could not withdraw in this evening of 24th owing to hostile barrage. HOR is made. HOR passed –	

WAR DIARY
INTELLIGENCE SUMMARY

Army Form C. 2118.

Place	Date	Hour	Summary of Events and Information	Remarks and references to Appendices
Schaft Farm	24-9-17		Guns arrived & laid on SOS lines. 2 Officers evacuated (frostbite jaw). Also 10R. 10R killed. 2nd Lt CW Watt took over his section. Temperature had for teasing work.	B22 b 2 2
	25.9.17		Lt Starling took over his section.	
	26.9.17		40,000 rounds brought up. Fire opened at 5.40 am & maintained for an hour, all guns. 24,000 rounds fired. 1 gun put out of action.	
	27-9-17		CO wounded, 2nd in Cmd took Command. 10R to hosp. Guns relaid on SOS lines. No casualties. Nos 3 & 4 Sections returned to Schickhoff Farm Rear HQ.	
	28.9.17		Nos 1 & 2 Sections " " "	
	29.9.17		Bty & Transport returned to Pitch Camp. Kit inspection & guns overhauled.	First 6 6 8 Shot - 24.
			Strength, beginning of month Off. 11 O.R. 177	
			do. End of month 8 165	
			Total Casualties, killed & wounded 4 25	
			Sick 9	
			Sick returned 5	
			Drafts received 2 12	

WM Crompton Lt.

59 M.G. Coy
Vol 20

Army Form C. 2118.

WAR DIARY
or
INTELLIGENCE SUMMARY.
(Erase heading not required.)

Instructions regarding War Diaries and Intelligence Summaries are contained in F. S. Regs., Part II. and the Staff Manual respectively. Title pages will be prepared in manuscript.

Place	Date	Hour	Summary of Events and Information	Remarks and references to Appendices
PROVEN AREA PILCH CAMP	30/9/17.		Church Parade for all.	F.15.b.8.8. (Sht. 27)
"	1/10/17.		Coy. and transport entrained and occupied camp early following morning near BEAULENCOURT.	N.16.a.14 (Sht. 57b)
BEAULEN-COURT.	2/10/17		Coy. inspected by C.O. Physical training.	"
"	3/10/17		do. Guns and ammunition cleaned.	"
"	4/10/17		Up to pressure of clothing and gun parts in order to proceed to EGYPT.	"
"			as a complete section.	
"	5/10/17		Lt. C.P. TANNER arrived from 100 Coy. to take command of this Coy. 2/Lt. W.H. MITCHELL and 2/Lt. D. McKENDRICK reported from France.	"
"			Lt. D.L. HOWARD work done – same as previous day.	
"	6/10/17		Coy. and transport proceeded to HEUDICOURT and occupied camp at W.15.b.5.4.	W.15.b.5.4.
"			Lt. STURZBURG and 2/Lt. R.R. JENNINGS with one complete section 59 M.G. Company	
HEUDICOURT	7/10/17		entrained at YTRES for the EAST via MARSEILLES at 5 a.m. Lt. TANNER 2nd Lt. LANE and 2nd Lt. McKENDRICK visited the line held by the 119th Brigade, and went round M.G. posters occupied by 119 M.G. Company. 59 M.G. Company relieved 119 M.G. Company in the centre sector of the Divisional front: relief complete by 10 p.m. without incident. Weather very wet.	O.O. No. 1.
In the Field.	8/10/17.		C.O. visited guns on the line. Very quiet day, still wet. 4 O.Rs reported from the Base	
In GOUZEAUCOURT.				

(A7092) Wt. W12859/M1293 75,000 1/17. D.D. & L., Ltd. Forms/C.2118/14.

Army Form C. 2118.

WAR DIARY
or
INTELLIGENCE SUMMARY.
(Erase heading not required.)

Instructions regarding War Diaries and Intelligence Summaries are contained in F. S. Regs., Part II. and the Staff Manual respectively. Title pages will be prepared in manuscript.

Place	Date	Hour	Summary of Events and Information	Remarks and references to Appendices
GOOZEACOURT	9/10/17		2nd in Command visited the guns. Everything quiet.	51 c SE R31 a 97
	10/10/17		Everything quiet.	
	11/10/17		O.M.G.O. and O.C. 31 M.G. Company visited guns with O.C. 31 M.G. Company.	
	12/10/17		20. O.Rs reported from the base.	
	13/10/17		Lieut. Howard resigned from Hospital. All quiet. nights very unsettled.	
	14/10/17		Indirect Fire carried out by No.1 Section on Cos. H.Q at R.9.b.00.40. 6750 rounds fired. at 10.p.m. and 11.10 p.m.	
	15/10/17		Indirect Fire by all the guns No 3 Section Rounds fired 1000. Weather fine.	
	16/10/17		Considerate shelling by enemy artillery. Roceawallas.	
	17/10/17		Indirect Fire with 3 guns. 2750 rounds fired.	
	18/10/17		Indirect Fire with 5 guns 12000 rounds fired; 2000 rounds fired by front line guns in support of a wire-cutting patrol.	
	19/10/17		Indirect Fire with 1 gun on BLEAK QUARRY from position in front of the Front Line. 3000 rounds fired.	
	20/10/17		All quiet. no firing.	
	21/10/17		10000 rounds fired at various targets. enfilade ment on CAMBRAI Rd. Heron-y-try.	
	22/10/17		Manoeuvres; no casualties. 5500 rounds. and various tasks. weather unsettled	

(A.0092). Wt. W12439/M1293. 75,000. 7/17. D.D. & L. Ltd. Forms/C.2118/14.

Army Form C. 2118.

WAR DIARY
or
INTELLIGENCE SUMMARY.
(Erase heading not required.)

Instructions regarding War Diaries and Intelligence Summaries are contained in F.S. Regs., Part II. and the Staff Manual respectively. Title pages will be prepared in manuscript.

Place	Date	Hour	Summary of Events and Information	Remarks and references to Appendices
GOUZEAUCOURT	23/10/17		Indirect fire on CORNER WORK 500 rounds fired.	MAP SHEET 57cSE R31.a.9.7
	24/10/17		Indirect fire at night 1500 rounds from 2 guns. All quiet.	
	25/10/17		Divisional Concentration: rounds fired 1000.	
	26/10/17		Indirect fire on Cambrai Rd and suspected Company H.Q. 500 rounds fired with sights.	
	27/10/17		Indirect fire on CORNER WORK with 2 guns in conjunction with Lt. Lt. T.Bn. Battery 197.5d. rounds fired. Batteries near Coy H.Q. heavily shelled.	
			all the morning. New emplacement started in FOSTER AVENUE. R.20.d.9.1.	
	28/10/17		Indirect fire with 3 guns. 1000 rounds fired; one gun fired 500 rounds	
			in reply to enemy snipers.	
	29/10/17		Two guns withdrawn from front line to positions on CAMBRAI Rd R.20.d.9.7.	
			in accordance with new Divisional Defence Scheme. Emplacement at R.20.d.9.1.	
			completed. Work on new emplacement at R20.c.5.4 continued.	
	30/10/17		Indirect fire with 4 guns on Junction of tracks R.16.a.65.45. 4100	
			rounds fired. I.O.R. wounded, slight.	
			Total Strength beginning of month. 4 14 9 162	
			end " " 4 1 4 23	
			Total Casualties sick wounded 3 36	
			Officers received 2	
			sick evacuated	
			Sent to trenches death.	

A.M. Crompton Lt. in Capt.
Comdg. 59 M.G. Coy.

War Diary
50th Machine Gun Coy
November 1917

WAR DIARY
or
INTELLIGENCE SUMMARY.
(Erase heading not required.)

Army Form C. 2118.

Instructions regarding War Diaries and Intelligence
Summaries are contained in F. S. Regs., Part II.
and the Staff Manual respectively. Title pages
will be prepared in manuscript.

Place	Date	Hour	Summary of Events and Information	Remarks and references to Appendices
GOUZEAUCOURT	31.10.17		Indirect fire on CAMBRAI ROAD (R 22 a 6.1 - R 22 a 40.95) - 6,000 rounds fired	R 31 a 90.25
Do.	1.11.17		Do. on CAMBRAI ROAD	do
			9,000 rounds fired.	do.
Do.	2.11.17		Indirect fire on Tracks, R 16 c 3.1 - 4,500 rounds fired	do.
Do.	3.11.17		Indirect fire on dump at R 4 d. 35. 15. 2,000 rounds fired	do.
			Indirect fire on CAMBRAI Road — 3000 rounds fired	do. to various
Do.	4.11.17		Indirect fire on M.G. Coy. and moved to	
Do.	5.11.17		Company relieved by 217 M.G. Coy. and moved to billets at HEUDICOURT (N 20 b. 80. 60)	W 20 b 50x
HEUDICOURT	6.11.17		Company kit inspection and gun deficiencies indicated for	do
Do.	7.11.17		Company inspection - gun drill, and gun drill for open warfare	do.
Do.	8.11.17		Company inspection by C.O. Close order drill and gun drill.	do.
Do.	9.11.17		Company inspection - Practice in laying guns by compass, and use of clinometer: also use of Vickers guns in open warfare.	do
Do.	10.11.17		Bisley trotho. Section drill and advanced gun drill	do
Do.	11.11.17		Church Service for all.	do

Army Form C. 2118.

WAR DIARY
or
INTELLIGENCE SUMMARY.

(Erase heading not required.)

Instructions regarding War Diaries and Intelligence Summaries are contained in F. S. Regs., Part II. and the Staff Manual respectively. Title pages will be prepared in manuscript.

Place	Date	Hour	Summary of Events and Information	Remarks and references to Appendices
HENDECOURT	12.11.17		Company moved up to Centre Sector relieving 217 M.G. Coy.	W20 b 80.60
CAGNICOURT	13.11.17		Indirect fire carried out on targets at Rd 70.75 and CAMBRAI Road	R31 a 70.35
			R22 a 6.2 – R23 a 40.95 – 7650 rounds fired.	
do	14.11.17		Indirect fire on SUNKEN RD. R16 a 10.30 to R10 c 40.10. 3750 rds. fired	do
do	15.11.17		Indirect fire on trenches at R16 c 3.1. – 2000 rounds fired. All available	do
			guns used. fired from 8 p.m. to 10.30 p.m. to cross ways of transport (23,000 rds.)	
do	16.11.17		Indirect fire on BUJAK HOUSE – 1750 rounds fired	do
do	17.11.17		Indirect fire on Road Junction at R14 b 6.2. 2000 rds. fired	do
do	18.11.17		Preparation made for Barrage positions about R20 c.	do
do	19.11.17		Above work completed and guns moved to Barrage emplacements	
	20.11.17			
	6.20 a.m.		In cooperation with the Artillery a barrage was fired by the Company on the HINDENBURG LINE in R9 and R10 from a position in R20 c. in support of a general attack by the III Corps. Length of Barrage 40 minutes: 30000 rounds fired.	O.O. No1.
	7.00 a.m.		Attack withdrawn to Green Line with field and supporting guns for sections to move forward with the infantry at at 23 hrs.	

WAR DIARY
or
INTELLIGENCE SUMMARY.
(Erase heading not required.)

Army Form C. 2118.

Place	Date	Hour	Summary of Events and Information	Remarks and references to Appendices
	20/11/17	9.50am	Lectins moved forward with 9th Inf. Brigade. No1 with 4th R.B. No3 with the 2nd Inz.	Hqd CREZEUCOURT Spare Sheet.
			Nos with 10th K.R.C. The advance was carried out with four casualties and sections established themselves by 3 A.M. as follows:	
		2/am	No1 Section in front of MASNIERES	
			No3 Section on a line running 6.27 Central – 6.33 Central – M.3.a. covering the CANAL and the high ground beyond.	
			Nos Section to 6.36.c with 10 K.R.R.C.	
	21/11/17		During the night so the infantry advanced EAST towards the BONAVIS – CREVECOEUR Spur, the guns were moved forward out on the morning were disposed as follows: – No 1 Section on the MASNIERES- CREVECOEUR road about 6.34.d. covering the cemetery and the rocket 6.34.f.1.9.	
			No3 Section in M.3.a. covering the top of the ridge in M.3.b.	
			No4 Section at the road junction 6.33.c.8.8. to cover the advance of the 10th K.R.R.C. on CREVECOEUR	
			No1 Section cased this advance with indirect fire from 6.34.c. and 25mm were pushed up to the cemetery during the night but withdrawn at daybreak.	

Army Form C. 2118.

WAR DIARY
or
INTELLIGENCE SUMMARY.

(Erase heading not required.)

Instructions regarding War Diaries and Intelligence Summaries are contained in F. S. Regs., Part II. and the Staff Manual respectively. Title pages will be prepared in manuscript.

Place	Date	Hour	Summary of Events and Information	Remarks and references to Appendices
Battlefield	22.11.17		No 3 and 4 Lewis Gun team maintained their position but Nos 1 and 2 withdrew under Battalion arrangements to reserve at G.32.b.	Sketch GOUZEAUCOURT first attack
		6.30 am	Company was relieved by 6o M.G. Coy and withdrew to following positions H.Q. and No 3 section to Brigade H.Q. at K.34.c.	
			No 1 Section to reserve position in R.6.a.	
			No 2 Section to a support position in G.31.b.	
	23.11.17		Sections remained in their positions.	
	24.11.17		Company withdrawn to Brigade reserve and bivouacked at GOUZEAUCOURT STATION.	
			Casualties during the operations as follows	
			Killed Pte T. M. All	
			Wounded 5 O.R.s	
GOUZEAUCOURT	25.11.17		Guns cleaned and all reserves steamed up in their	
	26.11.17		Making up reserves in guns and personal kit.	
	27.11.17		Inspection of sections by section officers.	
	28.11.17		Preparing reserves. Guns prepared for action.	

Army Form C. 2118.

WAR DIARY
or
INTELLIGENCE SUMMARY.
(Erase heading not required.)

Place	Date	Hour	Summary of Events and Information	Remarks and references to Appendices
Gouzeaucourt	29.11.17		Company proceeded to relieve 60 M.G. Coy in the line. Guns taken up by pack-mules. Total casualties during month:- Killed 1, Wounded 6, Sick 12. Became violent Sent returned 1 3	R31a 9d. 25.

Arth Crompton Lt.
59 M.C. Coy.

59th M.G. Coy

Army Form C. 2118.

WAR DIARY
or
INTELLIGENCE SUMMARY.
(Erase heading not required.)

M 22

Place	Date	Hour	Summary of Events and Information	Remarks and references to Appendices
Near Leuze Wood	30.	18-17	The Company, having taken up its position with 12 guns, was attacked at about 7 a.m. by a large number of enemy aeroplanes flying very low and firing down on them with M.G's. There was also a heavy bombardment of artillery which put out of action 3 of our guns. Some of the remainder of our guns was safely removed for anti-aircraft and infantry fire, but when the enemy infantry surfaced them from a very few yards away, they quickly removed their guns and joined in the withdrawing infantry. The O/c Company was on his way down to 60 Brigade H.Q. in the Sunken road when he was informed of the attack. He went out with the Serjt Major and all H.Q. men and took up a position in a trench where he found 2 machine guns without a team. He then learned whilst this gun had been firing to seek a better position since when he had been missing. The Serjt Major took over control and continued firing the gun until it was put out of action by a M.G.	(9 m.g. cas guns lost) M.G.C.

T2134. Wt. W708—776. 500000. 4/15. Sir J. C. & S.

WAR DIARY or INTELLIGENCE SUMMARY

Army Form C. 2118.

Place	Date	Hour	Summary of Events and Information	Remarks and references to Appendices
			Maillet. He then held that part of the trench for an hour with Lgnoka.	
			He and his men took up another position where they found 2 M.G's	
			with only one man in charge and removed them until 4 p.m.,	
			when he reported to an officer of 61 M.G. Coy. and worked under his	
			command until they were relieved 3 days later.	
			He lost the 12 guns, all of which were either knocked out of action or dis-	
			-abled before being left. Of 3 guns I have no information as none	
			of their teams have returned.	
			The 2nd in Command who was at Transport near HEUDICOURT was	
			given two guns and he, with the remainder of the men of the	
			Coy, proceeded to a position between the GOUZEAUCOURT – HEUDICOURT	
			Road and the GOUZEAUCOURT–FINS Road where he reported to the	
			G.O. of the 11th Bn. R.I.B. and took up two positions in a line	
			of trench which they were preparing. He remained there	
			until recalled to HEUDICOURT on the following afternoon.	
HEUDICOURT	2.12.17		The Company less by rail transport by road proceeded to RIBEMONT.	

SECRET.   54 M.G. Coy.   Copy No. 8   Nov. 15. 17.

Ref. /GOUZEAUCOURT   O. O. No. 4
    1/20.000.

1. **INTENTION** At a date to be notified later the 60th & 61st Brigades will attack & capture the HINDENBURG Line between CRINKET ROAD and the GOUZEAUCOURT-CAMBRAI Rd. The 59th Brigade will form a defensive flank facing East on the line of the Cambrai Rd.— M2d.9.7 — LES RUES VERTES.

2. **Role of M.G. Coy.**
   1. **Barrage**: Details have been already issued, and further instructions are contained in Appendix A.
   2. No. 3 Sect: (2/Lt. LOWE) with 10th R.B. on the Right.
      No. 1 Sect: (2/Lt. KENDRICK) with 11th R.B. on the Left.
      No. 4 Sect: (2/Lt. HOWARTH) with 10th K.R.R.C. in Support.
   The action of these Sections will be as laid down in Appendix B, but Section officers will keep close touch with Battn. Commanders, and the utmost boldness must be shown in pushing guns forward in order to exploit to the full any wavering on the part of the enemy.

3. **TIMES**
   The Barrage will be for 40 minutes. Exact times will be notified later. As soon as the BLUE LINE is taken, teams will be ready to move forward behind the infantry, who will advance in Artillery Formation.
   For Teams & Loads see Appendix C.

4. **Communication** will be by runner and by telephone, if possible; batten. signalling stations should be used where practicable.

5. **RATIONS & WATER**
   Two days' rations & 1 iron ration will be carried. These will be dumped on Z1 night at No. 1 Sect. H.Q. and collected by teams from there; each team will have 1 filled patrol tin.

6. Brigade H.Q. will be at R.19 d.2.6. until the BROWN LINE is taken and then at CORNER WORK.

7. Coy. H.Q. will move to FOSTER AVENUE on Z1 night, R20 d 78.15. and will be at R.5. central after the Defensive Flank has been established.

8. An aeroplane will be up continuously from daylight onwards on ZERO day: the approach of any hostile troops will be signalled by the dropping of a smoke bomb which will burst about 100 ft. below the machine or white parachute flare, which descends leaving a trail of brown smoke 1 foot broad behind it. On seeing this signal M.G. fire will be opened at once on all hostile approaches in the neighbourhood.

9. **Medical Arrangements**
   Aid Posts: Gun Pit Store in PARTRIDGE RD. Main Dressing Station GOUZEAUCOURT.

10. Zero Time will be notified later.

11. Transport: 12 mules with pack saddles will be at No. 1 Sect. H.Q. in FIFTEEN RAVINE at 0 + 50 mins; 4 mules & 4 drivers will be allotted to each section going forward.

12. WATCHES will be synchronized at Coy. H.Q. in POSTAR AVENUE at Zero — 4 hours.

13. ACKNOWLEDGE.

F.P. Tanner
Capt.

By Orderly
No. 1 Copy No. 1 Sect.
" 2 " No. 3 "
" 3 " " 4 "
" 4 " Brigade

No. 5 copy to D.M.G.O. O.C 59 M.G. Coy
No. 6 & 7 War Diary
No. 9 T.O.

APPENDIX A — BARRAGE ARRANGEMENTS

1. Time of fire — 40 mins.
2. Belt filling at A 4 position
3. Sections will take up positions as under:—
   No. 4 Left   E. 2/Lt. HOWARTH
   No. 1 Centre D. 2/Lt. McKENDRICK
   No. 3 Right   C. 2/Lt. LANE
4. Surplus stores will be returned to Transport lines on Y/Z night.
5. On conclusion of Barrage, gun teams will retire to GREEN LINE, clean and refill guns, refill belts and prepare to move with the Infantry.
6. 2 men with each gun; remainder in 15 RAVINE & GREEN LINE.
7. Surplus belt boxes & surplus petrol tins will be left at A 4 position in charge of one man and collected later by T.O. Gun, etc. for Barrage will be brought to gun positions on Y/Z night by 3.0 a.m. on ration limbers.
8. Breakfast will be prepared in 15 RAVINE and eaten before Zero.
9. Group Commanders will be responsible for keeping infantry outside the danger zone of guns in action.
10. 2 Petrol tins per gun will be required for cooling purposes; guns will be oiled after each belt, and barrels rubbed through after every 4 belts, and elevation and direction checked.
11. 1 Gun will keep up intermittent fire until 0 – 10 mins. to cover noise of assembling troops.

3.

APPENDIX B

Sections going forward will take up positions as under:

No. 3 Sect: 2 guns to about M 2 b 4.2. To fire N.E., cover the approaches from the Canal and the rising ground beyond. 2 guns to G 32 d., to cover the eastern exits from the village, and the approaches to crossings of the Canal.

No. 1 Sect: (2/Lt. McKENDRICK) 2 guns to about G 26 c 5.0., to cover the main road to MASNIERES and the western exits. 2 guns to about G 25 d Central, to cover the Bridge in G 19 and the woods in G 25. As soon as the situation is clear these 2 guns will be withdrawn to a position behind the strong point at L 29 d 80.00.

No. 4 Sect: (2/Lt. HOWARTH) 2 guns will be in support on either side of the valley in L 35 d 80.20. 2 guns will remain in Reserve at Coy. H.Q. at R 6 Central.

Mules will be taken as far forward as possible, but a dump will be established as soon as possible at about L 36 d 40.80.

APPENDIX C - TEAMS & LOADS

No. 3 Sect: (each team)	No. 4 Sect:	No. 1 Sect:
1 mule	1 mule	1 mule
4 M. Gunners	4 M. Gunners	4 M. Gunners
3 Carriers	1 N.C.O.	2 Carriers
1 N.C.O.	2 Carriers	1 N.C.O.
1 Driver	1 Driver	1 Driver

LOADS

Gun: Tripod: Water tin: Cleaning rod.
10 Belt boxes
2 Shovels
First aid case

Every man.

Pack
Waterproof Sheet
Mess tin
2 days rations
Iron rations
2 Sand-bags.

WAR DIARY
or
INTELLIGENCE SUMMARY.
(Erase heading not required.)

Army Form C. 2118.

Place	Date	Hour	Summary of Events and Information	Remarks and references to Appendices
			where they arrived at rest until the 6th when they proceeded to	
			EBIEF SAINS-LES-FRESSIN where they remained until the 11th	
			cleaning, packing up deficiencies and re-organising, when they	
			proceeded to CAMPAGNE-lès-Arras	
CAMPAGNE	12.12.17		Physical Training. Inspection of guns + equipment. Close order drill	S 30 C (Aug 27 SW)
	13.12.17		do. do. Machine guns + limbers Cleaning limbers	
	14.12.17		do. do. Machine limbers. Inspections	
	15.12.17		do. Inspection by C.O. Close order drill. Inspection Capts AN	
			Richardson arrived to take over command of the Bn. 2/Lt W. Dunlop also reported	
	16.12.17		Church Services.	
	17.12.17		Physical Training and Inspection of Bn. by D.D.G.C. Baths and	
			Gun Cleaning	
	18.12.17		Physical Training. Company firing on the range. 12,000 rounds.	
	19.12.17		Physical Training. Kit Inspection. Inspection of transport by C.O.	
			Section with section Officers	

Army Form C. 2118.

WAR DIARY
or
INTELLIGENCE SUMMARY.
(Erase heading not required.)

Instructions regarding War Diaries and Intelligence Summaries are contained in F. S. Regs., Part II. and the Staff Manual respectively. Title pages will be prepared in manuscript.

Place	Date	Hour	Summary of Events and Information	Remarks and references to Appendices
CAMPAGNE	20/12/17		Physical Training. Bath. killed. Section parades.	5.30.c
"	21/12/17		Physical Training. Section had range practice and revolver practice	(30.27) S.H.
"	22/12/17		Physical Training. One Section laid out and picked battery in limbers.	
"	23/12/17		Church Service	
"	24/12/17		Physical Drill and Bayonet practice	
"	25/12/17		Lewis Gunner. White Company dined together	
"	26/12/17		Physical Training. Saw full Hurley Company parade in swordstick	
"	27/12/17		Physical Training and Section parade	
"	28/12/17		do.	
"	29/12/17		Kit inspection and Physical Training	
"	30/12/17		Church Services. 2/Lt C.V. Nelson joined from Base	

Casualties
Killed — 6
Wounded — 1
Missing — 4
To Hospital — 56
— 2

Stoke wounded from Hospital — 6
— 70
— 1 — 4

L. M. Crompton Lt.

59th H. Col

WAR DIARY
or
INTELLIGENCE SUMMARY.
(Erase heading not required.)

Army Form C. 2118.

Place	Date	Hour	Summary of Events and Information	Remarks and references to Appendices
CAMPAGNE B1121.D			Company formed	Sheet 27 S.W.
"	1.1.18		Physical Training and Section practice. Inspection of men in full field dressing & identity discs. C.O. inspected all articles in charge of Section.	5 30 c.
"	2.1.18		Range Practice.	do
"	3.1.18		Physical Training and C.O.'s inspection of Company in marching order.	do
"	4.1.18		Inspection of Coy by G.O.C. Division. Coy. photographed by sections.	do
"	5.1.18		Physical Training and Section parades.	do
"	6.1.18		Transport moved to Line area. Staging at GODESWARSVELDE. On night	do
"	7.1.18		Company moved to DICKEBUSCH area by bus from EBBLINGHEM	do
LACLYTE	8.1.18		Physical Training. Open staff Fatigue done by Company. Packing etc.	BESTAQUET(Sheet 28) M60.5-9
"	9.1.18		Physical Training. All kit & mess examined and cleaned	do
"	10.1.18		Company fatted. CSM. C. NEWMAN awarded DCM for action at CAMBRAI.	do
"	11.1.18		Company relieved 40 B. Coy in the line. No 2 stacked showing MENIN ROAD Scene at 11.12.13.4 were in pillboxes and could not	EINA600

under Lt. THOMAS

Ainet

WAR DIARY
or
INTELLIGENCE SUMMARY.

(Erase heading not required.)

Army Form C. 2118.

Place	Date	Hour	Summary of Events and Information	Remarks and references to Appendices
Whytschaete	1917. 12		Coy relieved by day all ranks being under observation (N° 4 platoon	Lt Nicod
MENIN RD to dugouts	to 14		The Coy retreat[ed] noiselessly and be relieved all teams by 3 a.m.	
	14.		1 N.C.O. The enemy frequently shelled our tracks by night. His indirect M.G. fire was very annoying. We lost 13 guns in the line. Capt. & Officers 75 O.R. — LT. CROMPTON in charge.	
	14.		Capt. ANDERSON returned from flying Corps proceeded up the line relieving LT. CROMPTON. Itself the N.Z. platoon was relieved	
	15.		2/Lt TUKE proceeded on a 5 weeks TX Corp School Infantry Course.	
	17		Company relieved by 10th M.G. Coy in line. By casualty. Coy proceeded	
LA CLYTTE CAMP	to		LA CLYTTE CAMP. We lost during period 2000 O.R's 1 I fine	
	18		C.S.M. NEWMAN D.C.M. with Battn Hd Qrs. Coy cleared up, Coy training	
SNAPP.	23		Coy relieved to M.G. Coy in line. Dispositions & guns as before. The [illegible] condition & enemy morale much improved.	
			Capt. ANDERSON to O.C. 88 O.R. 2/Lt. NOLAN i/c. N° 1, 2, 3, 4 Guns.	
	24.		LT. CROMPTON proceeded on leave.	CmR

WAR DIARY
or
INTELLIGENCE SUMMARY.

(Erase heading not required.)

Army Form C. 2118.

Place	Date	Hour	Summary of Events and Information	Remarks and references to Appendices
LINE	29		Coy relieved in the line by 60 M.G. Coy. We had expended 36000 rds in Indirect Fire and had in conjunction with T.M. relieved all enemy traffic in M.Gs. that first ran the vicinity of MENIN Rd. — In consequence. Remove shoft of the enemy artillery had been much reduced and our relief was much easier +	
LA CLYTTE CAMP	30		Coy proceeded by train to LA CLYTTE CAMP. Coy cleaned kitted (3 pm to 5 pm).	
CAMP			Strength O.R's 1 Casualties Killed 20 Wounded 5 Reinforcements { 2 R.P.s 11 Runners } S.P.H.R.'s 13 Hewitts 9 From Hospital	

(signature) CAPT.
O.C. 59th M.G. COMPANY.

WAR DIARY
or
INTELLIGENCE SUMMARY.
(Erase heading not required)

Army Form C. 2118.

Place	Date	Hour	Summary of Events and Information	Remarks and references to Appendices
LA CLYTTE CAMP.	31.1.18	1.18 1.2.18	Physical training, Section Parade and improvements of Camp. Inspection by G.O.C. Brigade. Went out of the line in afternoon. Training in afternoon.	Sheet 2.8
In the line Menin Road Section.	4.2.18		Company relieved 60 M. G. Coy in the line. Rear Coy. H.Q. at CAFÉ Belge Camp, near Dickebusch. Thirteen guns went into the line, the 5th three Reserve guns were taken up taking over positions from 217 M. G. Coy. The 16 guns remained in the line for the duration of the tour. Two men were killed and while normal conditions were in the trenches two men were wounded by a shell and 6 men were wounded by dropping into the passage of their hill-bloc. The Sergeant died the same day. the 9th Coy man with this pack while starting a tunnel trip were the only casualties by a working party. These were Physical and Bayonet. 2.14. NOLAN proceeded on a Physical and Bayonet Training Course on 10th inst.	

Army Form C. 2118.

WAR DIARY
or
INTELLIGENCE SUMMARY
(Erase heading not required.)

Instructions regarding War Diaries and Intelligence Summaries are contained in F. S. Regs., Part II. and the Staff Manual respectively. Title pages will be prepared in manuscript.

Place	Date	Hour	Summary of Events and Information	Remarks and references to Appendices
	12.2.18		The Company was relieved in the line by 60 M.G.C. and returned to LA CLYTTE Camp.	Sheet 28
LA CLYTTE	13.2.18		Transport proceeded by march route to LYNDE	
"	14.2.18		The Company less transport entrained at DICKEBUSCH and detrained at EBBLINGHEM, billeting at HAZEBROUCK	Sheet
	15.2.18		LYNDE. Time devoted to Cleaning up, Range practice, and full inspections by C.O's stores to change of section, and inspection of body transport entrained at STEENBECQUE, detraining at NESLE, Company Amens spent at MAVENCOURT, the night was the next day E ESMERY - Company marching the next day to HALLOW, where the men N.G. Coy 23rd division was here until. On the 26th that billetting was moved again until the Company, until the 26th that was transferred to AVRICOURT. at MARGNY	Sheet 66 D

Army Form C. 2118.

WAR DIARY
or
INTELLIGENCE SUMMARY.
(Erase heading not required.)

Instructions regarding War Diaries and Intelligence Summaries are contained in F. S. Regs., Part II. and the Staff Manual respectively. Title pages will be prepared in manuscript.

Place	Date	Hour	Summary of Events and Information	Remarks and references to Appendices
AVRICOURT	27-2-18		Limbers cleaned. Inspection by Lt. CROMPTON. C.O. proceeded to XIX. Corps H.Q.	66 D.
			CASUALTIES	
			Killed — O/R's 3	
			Wounded. — 2	
			Hospital — 10	
			From Hospital — 3	
			Draft received — nil	

M. Hall Capt.
O. C. 59th M. G. COMPANY.

[Stamp: 11th (SERVICE) BATT. 3 APR 1918 KING'S ROYAL RIFLE CORPS]

1   LB32

HQ 20th Division.

Attach war diary for
the month of March 1918

A. Mackintosh
Capt & Adjt
6/4/18   for O.C. 11th K.R.Rifles

www.ingramcontent.com/pod-product-compliance
Lightning Source LLC
Chambersburg PA
CBHW081545160426
43191CB00011B/1844